Girl, Your Goal Is Jannah

Discover the transformative power of faith

Farhat Amin

Girl, Your Goal Is Jannah

By Farhat Amin

www.smartmuslima.com

WANT FREE

BONUS CONTENT?

SCAN ME NOW!

INTRODUCTION

Girl, finding your path to jannah can sometimes feel daunting in a world filled with distractions and challenges. But fear not; I have curated a collection of hadith and ayahs to guide you on your sacred journey.Step into a world where faith and determination are your guiding stars. 'Girl, Your Goal Is Jannah' offers a treasury of wisdom to inspire you helping you maintain focus on your most precious aspiration – jannah.

Brimming with thought provoking questions, a source of strength, and a reminder that your destination is within reach. Discover the transformative power of faith as you delve into Islam's profound teachings and choose to apply them in your daily life. 'Girl, Your Goal Is Jannah' is not just a book; it's a sanctuary for introspection, a trusted companion you can depend on when you need an iman boost. So, are you ready to embark on a transformative journey? Be inspired and equipped with valuable steps to keep moving forward. Join countless other Muslimahs on the path to jannah. Girl, your goal is clear, and this book is your roadmap.Inshallah, let's remember each other in our duas.

Your Sister, Farhat Amin
www.smartmuslima.com

"We created man—We know what his soul whispers to him: We are closer to him than his jugular vein" (50:16)

I n your quest for jannah, contemplate this verse deeply. It's a reminder, a heartfelt revelation that unveils the intimate connection between you and Allah. The Most Merciful, tells you that He created you, and not only that, but He knows the innermost whispers of your soul. Imagine that for a moment—the One who fashioned you knows the secrets of your heart, the thoughts you've never shared, and the emotions you've never expressed.

When He says, "We are closer to him than his jugular vein," He's emphasising His nearness, an intimacy that surpasses any human relationship. It's a closeness that cannot be measured physically because it transcends the material world. Think about your jugular vein—it's vital, unseen, and hidden within. Similarly, Allah's presence is essential, unseen by our eyes, yet deeply embedded within your existence.

Understanding this verse means recognising that you are never alone. In moments of joy, sadness, and even solitude, remember that He is with you, closer than anyone or anything else. Allow your awareness of Allah, taqwa, to guide your actions, thoughts, and intentions. Seek comfort in His closeness, and let it fuel your obedience to Him. Embrace the beautiful reality that He knows you better than you know yourself, and let that knowledge deepen your connection with Him.

Reflect on a moment when you felt a deep connection with your Creator. How did you achieve this?

....
....
....
....
....
....
....
....
....
....

Are there 'things' in your life that are hindering your mindfulness of Allah?

....
....
....
....
....
....
....

Consider ways in which you can release yourself from these hindrances.

....
....
....
....
....
....
....
....
....
....
....
....
....

As I journey toward jannah, I want to practise the following actions to enhance my consciousness of Allah.

....
....
....
....
....
....
....

"I have not created men except that they should worship Me." (Adh-Dhariyat, 51:56)

T ogether, let's unravel the essence of worship in Islam—a concept that may differ from what many think it to be. Islam offers a unique perspective. You see, Islam is not just a religion—it's a complete way of life. It encompasses a comprehensive set of laws and guidelines that touch every aspect of human existence. From personal and collective religious rituals to social matters, education, morals, economics, politics, and international relations, Islam guides how to navigate all facets of life with justice and virtue.

Worship in Islam goes beyond traditional rituals; it's a holistic approach. It's about loving Allah, seeking to please Him, truly knowing Him, and dedicating your actions to Him alone. Every word, every deed, and every interaction can become an act of worship when done with the intention of pleasing Allah. Without realising, you could be revering other than Allah, such as your desires or other people. Let's explore how this can occur.

Worshipping Desires

*   Material Obsession: When you constantly consume and seek wealth as your primary source of joy, your life becomes centred around unquenchable greed and the relent-

less need to display affluence. You never find contentment, and this pursuit can lead you to do anything to accumulate wealth. The growing popularity of platforms like OnlyFans is a disturbing example of this phenomenon.

- Hedonistic Pursuits: Engaging in self-indulgent behaviours, where instant gratification and pleasure take precedence, can lead us away from the path of worshipping Allah. We prioritise dopamine hits without considering the consequences.

- Addictive behaviours: Substance addictions, cannabis and alcohol, are well-documented. However, addictive behaviours extend beyond substances. Activities such as gambling, consumption of explicit content, and the relentless pursuit of online popularity can transform into forms of adoration. These addictions can exert profound control over our lives, redirecting our focus from seeking Allah's guidance and mercy to serving these insatiable desires.

Worshipping Other People

- Codependency: In personal relationships, we may unknowingly engage in codependent behaviour, relying excessively on someone else for our emotional well-being. This dependence can lead us to neglect our needs and values, ultimately placing the person above Allah.

- Idolisation: Sometimes, we idolise friends or celebrities, believing our happiness and purpose hinge solely on their approval or imitation. This can lead us to blindly follow them rather than the best person who walked the earth, our beloved Prophet Muhammad (saw).

Do you categorise some actions as worship, following Islamic guidelines, while leaving others to your own choice? Jot down examples.

....

....

....

....

....

....

....

....

....

....

....

....

Choose a specific daily action. Reflect on how you can transform it into an act of worship by intending to please Allah.

....

....

....

....

....

....

....

....

....

....

....

....

Girl, are there people in your life, online or in person, who are not helping you gain jannah? Be brave. Decide how you are going to reduce the toxic impact they have on you.

....

....

....

....

....

....

....

....

....

....

....

....

....

....

....

....

....

....

....

....

Do you think you are obsessed with the online world? To the point it's effecting your concentration in salah or how much Quran you read? Or generally how present you are with your family? Have you thought about taking breaks from your phone in the day?

....

....

....

....

....

....

....

....

....

....

....

....

....

"Abu Hurayrah narrated the Prophet (saw) informed us that 'Every child is born on 'fitrah' (the natural inclination to Islam); however, the child's parents make him a Jew or Christian. It is as an animal delivers a perfect baby animal. Do you find it mutilated?"(Muslim)

T his illuminating hadith reminds us of the inherent purity and natural inclination towards the truth we are born with. It's a reflection on the influence of our upbringing, including the pop culture, and schooling that our parents allowed us to access, in shaping our beliefs. Consider this: when you were born, your heart and soul were inclined towards the truth, towards the recognition of the one true God—Allah. It's as pure as the birth of a baby lamb. Yet, as you grew, your environment and the beliefs of those around you played a role in the path you eventually followed.Now, dear count your blessings that your parents raised you as a Muslim. But as an adult, you must continue nurturing your natural inclination towards Islam. If you are a revert, be grateful to Allah for guiding you back to the truth.

Remember, there is always time to reconnect with your fitrah, your innate disposition towards Islam. Reflect on your journey, seek knowledge from people of knowledge, not TikTokkers or liberal Muslims, and strive to align your beliefs and actions with the pure fitrah with which you were born. Let this hadith lead you to introspection. In the West, the education system actively promotes secu-larism, LGBTQ ideology and feminism. All of which contradict Islam.

Sis, do you think it's possible that some unnatural beliefs about gender, sexuality and personal freedom have crept into your psy-che? Jot down your thoughts.

....
....
....
....
....
....
....
....
....
....
....

Reflect on the role of upbringing and culture in shaping your faith and beliefs. Is there a specific practice in your upbringing that con-tradicts Islamic tradition?

....
....
....
....

....
....
....
....
....
....
....
....
....
....
....
....
....
....
....
....

If so, consider how to free yourself from this conflicting practice
with your commitment to Islam.

....
....
....
....
....
....
....
....

Abu Dharr reported: The Messenger (saw), said, "Allah Almighty says: Whoever comes with a good deed will have the reward of ten like it and even more. Whoever comes with an evil deed will be recompensed for one evil deed like it or he will be forgiven. Whoever draws close to Me by the length of a hand, I will draw close to him by the length of an arm. Whoever draws close to Me by the length of an arm, I will draw close to him by the length of a fathom. Whoever comes to Me walking, I will come to him running. Whoever meets Me with enough sins to fill the earth, not associating any partners with Me, I will meet him with as much forgiveness." (Saḥiḥ Muslim)

SubhanAllah! Can you grasp the immense magnitude of Allah's generosity? When you sincerely perform a good deed, Allah multiplies the rewards manifold, going beyond what we can even fathom. And when you commit a mistake, a sin, Allah, in His boundless mercy, offers you the chance for forgiveness, wiping away your transgression.

But there's more. Imagine the closeness and intimacy that Allah offers you when you take that first step towards Him. As you inch closer to Him, He rushes to you with His infinite grace, extending His mercy far beyond what you could have imagined. This hadith illustrates the unmatched love and compassion our Creator has for His devoted servants.

And remember this, my dear no matter how vast your sins may seem, as long as you approach Allah with sincerity, never associating partners with Him, His forgiveness is boundless. His mercy encompasses all, and His love for His servants knows no bounds. So, don't let your past sins be a barrier to turning to Allah. Repent. Learn from your mistakes. Keep moving forward. May Allah guide and bless you on your path to jannah.

Take a moment to consider what obstacles hinder your connection with Allah: personal struggles, doubts, or external pressures?

....

....

....

....

....

....

....

....

....

....

....

....

....

....

....

....

....

....

....

Once you've identified these barriers, contemplate how to address them. Take one at a time.

....

....

....

....

....

....

....

....

....

....

What steps can you take to remove these obstacles and create a stronger and more meaningful connection with Allah? Remember that self-awareness and sincere reflection can be the first steps toward positive change and a deeper spiritual connection.

....

....

....

....

....

....

....

....

....

....

....

Recall a time when you sincerely sought forgiveness from Allah. Describe the circumstances and emotions you felt during that moment of repentance.

....

....

....

....

....

....

....

....

....

....

....

....

....

Abdullah ibn Amr reported: The Prophet (saw) said, "Rejoice! Rejoice! Verily, whoever performs the five prayers and avoids the major sins will enter paradise from whichever gate he wishes." Ṭabarani

Jannah is not a distant dream but a tangible reality, achievable through steadfast acts of worship and righteousness. You're paving a direct route to paradise as you faithfully perform your daily prayers and conscientiously shun major sins. The gates stand ajar, and it is you who selects the entrance. I'm sure you are thinking, wouldn't it be wise to find out what the major sins are to steer yourself away from them? This hadith outlines seven major sins, but there are more. Inshallah, commit to researching all of them; it won't take long.

Abu Huraira reported: The Prophet (saw) said, "Stay away from seven major sins." They said, "O Messenger of Allah, what are they?" The Prophet said, "Idolatry with Allah, occult magic, killing a soul that Allah has sanctified except for a just cause, consuming usury, usurping the property of an orphan, fleeing the battlefield, and accusing chaste believing women." Bukhāri & Muslim

I'm going to research the major sins by...................................
....
....

....

....

....

....

....

Do you struggle with praying your salah? Why do you think that is?

....

....

....

....

....

....

....

....

....

....

....

....

....

....

....

What practical actions can you do to help yourself pray regularly?

....

....

....

....

....

....

....

....

Here are some ideas. Download a salah app. Go to bed early so you don't miss fajr. Put your alarm away from your bed. Ask your family to wake you up. Write your plan of action!

....

....

....

....

....

....

....

....

....

....

....

....

....

....

....

....

Ibn Abbas reported: The Messenger of Allah (saw) said, "Take advantage of five before five: your youth before your old age, your health before your illness, your riches before your poverty, your free time before your work, and your life before your death." Bayhaqi

L et's mull over the wisdom conveyed in the words of the Messenger of Allah (saw) as he shares guidance that transcends time and speaks directly to the heart of our existence.The Prophet (saw) invites us to seize five critical opportunities before they fade away.

Youth is a period of peak cognitive ability, zeal, and sharpness; cherish it. By the way nowadays forty is still considered young! Pursue knowledge, strengthen your faith, and hone your talents. Spend your energy on activities enriching your akhirah and bringing you closer to Allah.

Good health is an invaluable blessing that often escapes our appreciation until it is compromised. Maintain your physical and mental well-being with gratitude. This is the vessel through which you worship, serve others, and fulfil your purpose. Nurture it through healthy eating, reading, reduce screen time, exercise and self-care.

Wealth is a means, not an end. Use your money to alleviate the suffering of those less fortunate, support noble causes, and cultivate generosity. Your wealth is a trust from Allah, so use it to earn His pleasure. Don't waste your money buying things you don't need. TikiTok can't make you buy anything; the choice is yours.

Time is a currency we can never replenish. Prioritise your days to include moments of reflection, worship, and self-improvement. Guard your time from binging Netflix and mindlessly scrolling Instagram. It's in these pockets of free time that your soul can flourish.

Life is a transient journey, and none possesses a guarantee of its duration. Embrace each day as an opportunity for spiritual growth and acts of kindness. Remember that the legacy you leave behind is what will take you to jannah or jahannum. My dear sister, the Prophet's words are a timeless reminder of the fragility and preciousness of life's moments. They beckon you to be conscious of your choices, live purposefully, and minimise regrets.

Consider one change you can incorporate into the way you allocate your money that will contribute positively to your hereafter.

....

....

....

....

....

....

Reflect on a single adjustment you can introduce into your daily routine that will yield lasting benefits for your akhira.

....

....

....

....

....

....

....

....

....

....

....

....

....

....

....

Do you find yourself spending too much time on your phone?

....

....

....

....

....

....

....

. . . .

. . . .

. . . .

Perhaps you've got a handle on your social media use, but if you're struggling to break free from mindless scrolling, why not find three strategies to help you reduce this unproductive habit?

. . . .

. . . .

. . . .

. . . .

. . . .

. . . .

. . . .

. . . .

. . . .

. . . .

. . . .

. . . .

. . . .

. . . .

. . . .

. . . .

Abu Mūsa al-Ash'ari narrated the Prophet (saw) said: "The example of a believer who recites the Qur'an is like that of a citron; it smells good and tastes good. While the believer who does not recite the Qur'an is like a date, which has no smell and is good in taste. And the example of a hypocrite who recites the Qur'an is like a sweet basil; it tastes bitter but smells good. And the example of a hypocrite who does not recite the Qur'an is like the colocynth, which has no smell and tastes bitter." Bukhari

The Prophet (saw) vividly describes how our engagement with the Quran defines our essence.Like a fragrant and flavourful citron, a believer who recites the Quran is adorned with its beauty. Their recitation is not merely an exercise of the tongue but a fragrance that permeates their soul. The Quran's guidance infuses their life with purpose and goodness.

Although a date is sweet and nourishing, it lacks the aroma of the citron. Similarly, a believer who doesn't engage with the Quran may still possess goodness, but they miss out on the spiritual fragrance and depth of Quranic study.

Just as sweet basil may smell enticing but taste bitter, a hypocrite who recites the Quran may appear righteous on the surface but lacks sincerity. Their recitation doesn't align with their intentions.

The colocynth, with neither smell nor taste, is a stark symbol of emptiness. Similarly, a hypocrite who neglects the Quran remains spiritually barren, devoid of the Quran's fragrance and guidance.

Consider where you stand in this analogy. Strive to be like the citron—imbued with the Quran's beauty and wisdom. Let its recitation be a transformative experience that shapes your character and actions. In doing so, you will truly embody the essence of a believer, making the Quran an essential part of your life.

How can you improve your relationship with the blessed words of Allah?..

....

....

....

....

....

....

....

....

....

....

....

....

....

"Blessed is the One in Whose Hands rests all authority. And He is Most Capable of everything. He is the One Who created death and life in order to test which of you is best in deeds. And He is the Almighty, All-Forgiving." (67:1)

Society, friends and family can sometimes make it challenging to adhere to our faith. Peer pressure, societal norms, and the constant bombardment of distractions may sway us from the path of Islam. But it's essential to remember the long-term goal—the promise of everlasting paradise.

Our beloved Prophet Muhammad ﷺ and his companions faced immense challenges: ridicule, boycott and physical abuse. But they persevered, focusing on the eternal reward that awaited them in the hereafter. They understood that the trials of this world are temporary, but the joys of paradise are everlasting.

So, in the face of adversity and societal pressures, remember the eternal promise of Allah. Stay steadfast in your faith, uphold your principles, and strive for excellence in your deeds. When you encounter difficulties, do dua, envision the eternal paradise that awaits those who remain committed to the path of Islam. Let this verse be a guiding light, reminding you that the challenges of this world are but a fleeting test. Keep your gaze fixed on the long-term goal, and may it inspire you to navigate life's trials with unwavering faith and patience.

Think about a challenging experience you've had in the past.

....

....

....

....

....

....

....

....

....

....

....

....

With the benefit of hindsight, what lessons or insights did you gain from that experience?

....

....

....

....

....

....

....

Abu Musa narrated : Allah's Messenger (ﷺ) said, "The example of a good companion (who sits with you) in comparison with a bad one, is like that of the musk seller and the blacksmith's bellows (or furnace); from the first you would either buy musk or enjoy its good smell while the bellows would either burn your clothes or your house, or you get a bad nasty smell thereof." Bukhari

Imagine having a good friend as a soothing fragrance, like musk. When you're with them, the air is filled with a delightful scent. They inspire you, guide you, and make you feel at peace.

On the other hand, think of a bad companion as a hot, smoky furnace. Being around them can feel uncomfortable, like inhaling a foul smell. They will nudge you towards choices and habits that are harmful to your well-being in this life and the next.

So, my dear sister, remember the wisdom in this hadith. Just as you choose your favourite perfume, choose your friends carefully. Surround yourself with those who uplift your spirit, encourage your faith, and help you connect with Allah. These friends are like the soothing scent of musk, constantly enhancing your life. And if you find yourself in the company of those who steer you away from your faith or principles, it's okay to distance yourself.

Just as you would step away from a smoky furnace to protect yourself from harm, choose to step away from their unhealthy influence.In life's journey, you have the power to shape your surroundings. There is nothing wrong with being alone. Seek friends who nurture your soul, strengthen your confidence as a Muslimah, and encourage you to love Allah. Inshallah, you'll find peace and tranquillity in your heart with the right friends.

Who inspires your faith?

....

....

....

....

....

....

....

....

Who leads you toward negative choices?

....

....

....

....

....

....

....

....

....

....

....

....

What qualities do you want in friends who encourage your faith
and inspire personal growth?

....

....

....

....

....

....

....

If you have few 'musk sellers' in your life, how can you actively
seek out and find more of them?

....

....

....

....

....

....

....

....

....

....

"Cleanliness is half the faith (Iman)." Sahih Muslim

P ractically speaking, this hadith implies that cleanliness isn't just a hygiene routine; it's a profound part of your faith. It signifies purity, both in the physical and spiritual sense. Start with the basics: perform your wudu and ghusl with mindfulness, ensuring that every part of your body is cleansed before your acts of worship. This physical purification is not a mundane ritual but a spiritual preparation that brings you closer to Allah.

Maintain personal hygiene with diligence. The Prophet (saw) encouraged brushing your teeth, taking regular baths, and keeping your body and clothes clean. This reflects not only respect for yourself but also consideration for those around you.Beyond the physical realm, consider the cleanliness of your heart and intentions. Rid your heart of grudges, envy, and ill thoughts. Embrace forgiveness, compassion, and gratitude. Keep your intentions pure in all your actions, seeking Allah's pleasure alone.

In your daily routine, be mindful of how clean you keep your surroundings. Keep your bedroom, bathroom, kitchen, shared living spaces clean and free of clutter. The Prophet (saw) said, *"Allah is pure and loves purity."* (Tirmidi) By maintaining cleanliness and order, you contribute to a clutter free, organised life. No one likes mess, or having to clean up after other people. So be responsible.

Are you giving cleanliness the attention it deserves in your daily routine?

....
....
....
....

Would you describe yourself as messy or neat? Are you considerate towards your family when it comes to cleaning up after yourself?

....
....
....
....
....
....
....
....

Here are some suggestions to help you take control of your cleanliness. Put them into your calendar and make it part of your routine. Make the intention to hoover your room once a week, especially if you have a cat. Empty the bins. Wash your laundry three times a week. Donate clothes you don't wear to charity if you have too many clothes. Refrain from hoarding old things that you no longer use. I'm sure you have seen shows where people's rooms look like a bomb landed because they buy too much stuff and can't find anything. Inshallah, if you don't want to be held hostage by your clutter, you must be proactive and clean up!

"Indeed, your own self has rights over you." Abu Dawud

In your journey through life, don't overlook one fundamental aspect: your own self, your body, has rights over you. This isn't a suggestion; it's a truth embedded in the teachings of Islam.You see, your well-being, both physical and mental, is not a luxury but a responsibility. Neglecting it isn't just a disservice to yourself but a breach of those very rights. Your body is a trust given to you by Allah, and it's your duty to care for it.

When you read the hadith that states, "Indeed, your own self has rights over you," understand that it's a divine reminder of your obligation. It's a call to prioritise your physical and mental health because they are essential elements of your faith and life.

Physical health isn't merely about aesthetics or strength; it's about ensuring your body functions optimally. It means eating well, staying active, and avoiding harm to your body. Neglecting your physical health can lead to an inability to fulfil your duties as a servant of Allah.

Girl, your mental health is crucial. Your mind, emotions, and thoughts deserve attention. Don't let stress, anxiety, or negativity consume you. Seek help when needed, for a healthy mind contributes to a healthy heart and soul.Remember, caring for your body and mind isn't selfish; it's an act of worship. It allows you to serve Allah and fulfil your roles in life more effectively. So, honour the rights your body has over you, and in doing so, you'll strengthen your connection with your Creator and live a more fulfilling, purpose-driven life.

Please take a moment to evaluate your current self-care practices, both physically and mentally. Are there areas in your life where you've been neglecting your well-being? Do you eat healthy meals and exercise?

....

....

....

....

....

....

....

....

....

....

....

....

....

....

....

Are there obstacles or challenges in your life that have hindered your ability to care for your body and mind properly?

....
....
....
....
....
....
....
....
....
....
....
....
....
....
....

How can you prioritise self-care to fulfil your responsibility to your body and mind following Islamic teachings?

....
....
....
....
....
....

Prophet Muhammad (saw) said in Sahih al-Tirmidhi, "Increase your supplications for me in the last part of the night and after every obligatory prayer. Whoever blesses me at these times, his supplication is preserved by the angels till the Day of Judgment."

A mid life's storms, when our hearts are heavy with worry and our minds entangled in the webs of anxiety, salawat serves as a beacon of tranquillity. The act of sending blessings upon the Prophet Muhammad (saw) has a profound calming effect on the soul. As we send salawat, we are reminded of his timeless compassion; in that remembrance, we find solace.

The Prophet (saw) himself prescribed this spiritual remedy for us. He said, *"Increase your supplication for me in abundance on Fridays and in the last part of the night. Whoever blesses me once, Allah blesses him tenfold." (Sahih al-Bukhari)*

Transliteration of the Salawat:
Sending salawat is a simple yet powerful act. The most common form is:
"Allahumma salli 'ala Muhammadin wa 'ala ali Muhammadin, kama sallaita 'ala Ibrahim wa 'ala ali Ibrahim, innaka Hamidun Majid. Allahumma barik 'ala Muhammadin wa 'ala ali Muhammadin, kama barakta 'ala Ibrahim wa 'ala ali Ibrahim, innaka Hamidun Majid."

This beautiful salawat translates to: "O Allah, send Your blessings upon Muhammad and upon the family of Muhammad, as You sent Your blessings upon Ibrahim and upon the family of Ibrahim; You are indeed Praiseworthy and Glorious. O Allah, bless Muhammad and the family of Muhammad, as You blessed Ibrahim and the family of Ibrahim; You are indeed Praiseworthy and Glorious."

As you recite these words, let your heart be filled with love and reverence for the Prophet Muhammad (saw). Find comfort in knowing that your anxieties can be eased through this simple act of devotion. The salawat is not just a collection of words but a channel through which we connect with the Prophet's radiant example.

It is a means to invoke Allah's peace and blessings upon the one who brought us the light of Islam. In the salawat's embrace, we find spiritual elevation and a soothing balm for our anxious hearts.

How will you incorporate salawat into your daily routine?

....
....
....
....
....
....
....
....
....

"Who is most deserving of good care for me?' The Prophet replied, 'Your mother.' Then the man asked and who after that? He repeated, 'Your mother.' The man asked, 'And who after that?' the Prophet repeated, 'Your mother and then your father, then your nearest relatives in order of closeness." Bukhari

In your journey as a believer, this hadith should serve as a powerful compass for your conduct, in how you treat your mother. The words spoken by our beloved Prophet (saw) are not a coincidence or a random choice of words; they are a deliberate emphasis on the unparalleled status of your mother in Islam. The effect of this hadith on your life should be profound. It should ignite a fire of gratitude and compassion within your heart.

Your mother, who carried you in her womb, endured pain and discomfort for your sake, and nurtured you with her love and care, deserves your utmost respect and kindness. She holds a unique position in your life that no one else can claim. If you are a mother, teach your kids this hadith. This hadith should guide your treatment of your mother and your children's treatment of you. It means listening to your mother, assisting her, and showing her gratitude. It means making her comfort and well-being a priority in your life. Remember, it's not just about duty but love and honour. Your mother's rights over you are immeasurable, and recognising this truth is a cornerstone of your faith.

Be honest, do your treat your mother well? Jot down 3 ways you practically show kindness and gratitude to your mother.

....
....
....
....
....
....
....
....

If you do have problems with your mother, what do you think is the cause of them?

....
....
....
....
....
....
....
....
....
....
....
....
....
....

How can you begin to improve your relationship with your mother? No one is saying mums are perfect, but what can you do from your side to create a positive change?

....

....

....

....

....

....

....

....

....

....

If your mother has mistreated or abused you, how can you find a way to speak to her so you can heal from your trauma? Is there a family member who she would listen to who can facilitate your discussion?

....

....

....

....

....

....

....

....

"There is no obedience to anyone if it is disobedience to Allah. Verily, obedience is only in good conduct."
Bukhari

Remember this essential truth: obedience is not absolute; it is defined by the boundaries set by Allah. These boundaries are your guiding light, your moral compass in a world that often blurs the lines between right and wrong. Our beloved Prophet Muhammad (saw) illuminated a crucial principle: obedience should never lead you away from obedience to Allah. It is a reminder that your ultimate allegiance lies with the Creator.

In the face of any command or request, evaluate its alignment with the principles of Islam. It is your right, your responsibility, to discern whether an act is in harmony with Allah's guidance. If it veers into disobedience, then your obedience must be to Allah alone.This principle transcends cultural norms and parental desires. It reaffirms your commitment to living a life that is pleasing to your Lord, even if it means standing against the tide of popular opinion.

In essence, it's a call to uphold the highest standards of character and conduct, rooted in faith and unwavering commitment to Allah's commands. Your obedience is a reflection of your deep reverence for Him, and it should shine through in and it should shine through in your actions, choices, and interactions.

Remember, dear sister, if anyone—be it your parents, husband, or even the leader of your country—asks you to commit an act that goes against Allah's commands, you are not obligated to obey them in that matter. Your loyalty to Allah must always come first. Your obedience is a means of seeking His pleasure, and it is through such unwavering commitment that you find your true purpose.

So, let this truth guide you in your journey—a journey where obedience to Allah's decrees is the foundation of your faith, and your unwavering commitment to good conduct is a declaration of your love for your Creator.

Consider an instance in your life where you've had to make a choice between obedience to Allah or an authority figure. What did you choose? How did you feel about the choice you made?

....

....

....

....

....

....

....

....

....

....

....

Do you need help to make changes to create a mindset of obedience to Allah? Who are you going to turn to to get support?

....

....

....

....

....

....

....

....

Standing up to overbearing people can be challenging. Do dua to Allah to help you. Allah gave Asiya, the wife of Pharoah jannah, for standing up to him. Speak to Allah, ask Him for help, write your dua here.

....

....

....

....

....

....

....

....

....

....

....

"The one who does a bad deed shall be recompensed to the extent of the bad deed done, and the one who is a believer and does good deeds, whether man or woman, shall enter paradise and therein receive sustenance without measure." (Al-Ghafir, 40:40)

This verse isn't just a promise; it's crystal clear. It's a reminder that actions have consequences, and there's no escaping the scale of justice. Your wrongdoings will be weighed against the extent of the bad deeds committed. But there's hope here. Hope that radiates from belief and goodness. It's the hope that transcends gender, making it clear that paradise is not an exclusive club. Whether you're a man or a woman, belief and good deeds pave the path to a paradise beyond imagination.

Imagine a realm where your heart finds unending peace, your soul is perpetually content, and sustenance flows without bounds. It's a paradise where your faith and deeds open the doors to everlasting joy. Hold on to your belief fiercely in a world that often obscures the clarity of truth. Let it ignite your actions; let it guide your intentions. Your faith and good deeds are your currency for the hereafter, and their value is beyond measure.

No matter how small, every good act is a step towards an eternal abode of limitless sustenance. Your journey to paradise is not a distant dream; it's a reality awaiting your arrival.

Are you putting your soul first in your daily activities? For example your salah, being honest, keeping your promises, wearing hijab correctly, earning a halal income, calling out injustice?

....

....

....

....

....

How can you make the teachings within the Quran and Sunnah more pivotal in your life?

....

....

....

....

....

....

....

....

....

What must change for things to improve?

....

....

....

....

....

"Abu Hurayrah reported that the Prophet ﷺ said: 'Allah does not look at your bodies or at your forms; rather, He looks at your hearts and deeds." Sahih Muslim

In the grand design of creation, Allah has bestowed your face and body upon you. It is a trust from Him, a vessel for your soul in this worldly journey. Taking care of ourselves, including our physical well-being, is a responsibility.

But let us tread carefully along this path, for there's a fine line between taking care of ourselves and becoming consumed by our looks. People care about how 'pretty, thin or fair' you are and you can end up tailoring your appearance to garner compliments. In this age where societal pressures and media often glorify superficial beauty, it's essential to remember the bigger picture.

Yes, we should nourish our bodies with wholesome food and maintain our physical health. Exercise, eat well, and strive to live a balanced life that pleases Allah. These are acts of worship when done to fulfil the trust He has placed upon us.

However, let us not become ensnared by the obsession with appearances. Remember that we all age, and the passage of time will inevitably bring changes to our appearance. Wrinkles will form, hair will turn grey, and our looks will fade.

But herein lies a profound truth: your worth extends far beyond the boundaries of youth and physical beauty. It's in your character, good deeds, compassion, and faith. These attributes will stand the test of time, for they reflect the radiance of your soul. So, nurture your body as a trust from Allah, but do not allow it to define your identity or self-worth. Let your inner beauty, guided by faith and good deeds, shine forth and illuminate your path.

How important is your beauty to you?

....
....
....
....
....
....

Do you spend a lot of time and worrying about your looks? Do you spend a lot of money trying to conform to unrealistic beauty standards?

....
....
....
....
....
....
....
....

Do you feel unconfident or unattractive if you aren't wearing make-up? Think about why you feel that way? What influences in your life are making you feel ugly? Why should they have that power over you?

....
....
....
....
....
....
....
....
....
....
....

Who or what can you let go of that will help you focus less on your looks and more on your good deeds?

....
....
....
....
....
....
....
....

"Did you think that We had created you in play (without any purpose) and that you would not be brought back to Us?" (Al-Mumenoon, 23:115)

This verse invites you to pause and think about the purpose of your existence. Do you believe you were created for no reason or higher meaning? Do you think this life is pointless with no accountability?

Allah, the Most Merciful, has created you with a profound purpose. To live a god-conscious life. To learn about your deen. To advise your fellow Muslims. To invite others to Islam. To be the voice of the oppressed. Your life is not without meaning. It's a journey to the next life. And, yes, you are going to die one day. You need to prepare for death; don't avoid thinking about it. On the Day of Judgment, you will be asked about what you did in this life.

This awareness should make you mindful of Allah, knowing that every action, every choice, and every interaction holds weight. On that Day of Judgment, you will be held accountable for your deeds, which should serve as a powerful motivation to live a life that pleases Allah.

Treat people with kindness and give them their Islamic rights, for mistreating others and engaging in what is forbidden (haram) will have terrible consequences: jahanum. Just as Allah is the Most Merciful, He is also the Just. So, embrace life's journey with taqwa, seek to fulfil your purpose, and remember that you are destined to return to your Creator and be asked about your actions.

Are you looking forward to the moment when your deeds will be read out on the Day of Judgment?

....
....
....
....
....
....
....
....
....
....
....
....

Who has the most influence over you? Your friends, TikTokers, Youtubers, Netflix or Allah and His Messenger (saw)?

....
....
....
....
....
....

....

....

....

....

....

What content are you consuming that is not good for your soul?
Who do you need to unfollow?

....

....

....

....

....

....

....

....

....

It's never too late to make changes in your life to increase your
good deeds. Write down one change you can make today.

....

....

....

....

....

....

....

....

"Every son of Adam commits sin, and the best of those who commit sin are those who repent." Sunan Ibn Majah

You, are not exempt from committing sins. It's a universal truth that every child of Adam, including you, sometimes falls short. But here's the beautiful part: the best among those who sin are those who repent.Now, think about that for a moment. Repentance is a powerful concept in Islam. It's not just about admitting your mistakes; it's about acknowledging your imperfection as a human and turning back to Allah with sincerity and a desire for His forgiveness.

Repentance is a gift, a chance to cleanse your soul and draw closer to Allah. It's a reminder that no matter how many wrong turns you've taken, you can make a U-turn toward righteousness. Shaitan's tactics are cunning and relentless. He seeks to distance you from Allah's mercy, to make you believe that you are unworthy of the company of believers, and to keep you away from the gatherings of faith. But remember this: his whispers are the very chains he uses to bind you.

Refuse to be shackled by doubt and self-judgment. You are a beloved creation of Allah, and your return to Him is always within reach. Raise your hands in dua and seek His forgiveness, for His mercy knows no bounds.

Don't let Shaitan's deceptions lead you astray. Instead, heed the wisdom of our beloved Prophet Muhammad (saw). His guidance is a flashlight in the darkness, showing you the way back to Allah's infinite love and grace. Let his example inspire you to overcome the whispers of doubt and embrace the path of repentance.

Research how to do sincere repentance and follow the steps.

....

....

....

....

....

....

....

....

....

....

....

....

....

How do you protect yourself from the whispers of Shaitan?

....

....

....

....

....

....

....

....

....

....

In general before doing an action do you check if it is allowed?

....

....

....

....

....

....

....

....

Do you have knowledgable people that you can ask for guidance? If you don't jot down how you are going to actively find them.

....

....

....

....

....

....

....

....

....

....

....

Yazid ibn Asad reported: The Messenger of Allah (saw) said to me, 'O Yazid, love for people what you love for yourself.' In another narration, the Prophet (saw) said, 'Do not treat people but in the way you would love to be treated by them."(Ahmad)

Dear sister, let's journey into the core of our faith, where compassion and empathy reside. Our beloved Prophet Muhammad (saw) gifted us a timeless principle: "Love for people what you love for yourself." In simpler words, treat others exactly as you would want to be treated.

Imagine a world where every soul lived by this profound wisdom. It's a world where kindness and understanding flow freely, where respect and empathy reign supreme. Yet, in our complex lives, we often overlook this simple, golden rule.

Reflect on this for a moment: How would you want to be treated in various situations? With kindness, respect, and fairness, I presume. This, dear sister, is precisely how you should interact with others.

Let these words guide your actions. When you encounter people from diverse walks of life, remember the Prophet's words. Whether it's a neighbour, a colleague, a stranger, or even someone you may disagree with, let your conduct be a reflection of your own desires.

The essence of Islam lies in these teachings, where the beauty of character is illuminated. It's about forging connections, fostering understanding, and building a world where everyone feels valued.

So, as you navigate your path, let this principle be your compass. When you encounter differences, let empathy be your guide. When you meet hardship, let kindness be your response.

Think of a situation where you had a significant difference in opinion with someone close to you, such as a family member or friend. How did this difference impact your ability to treat them as you would want to be treated? What specific challenges did you face in maintaining empathy and kindness in that situation?

....
....
....
....
....
....
....
....
....
....
....
....
....

How did this difference impact your ability to treat them as you would want to be treated? What specific challenges did you face in maintaining empathy and kindness in that situation?

....
....
....
....
....
....
....
....

Reflect on any instances where you may have held prejudices or biases against certain individuals or groups. How did these biases affect your ability to treat those individuals with fairness?

....
....
....
....
....
....
....
....
....
....
....

....

....

....

....

....

....

....

Consider the barriers you faced in overcoming such biases and how you can work toward eliminating them to better practice the golden rule.

....

....

....

....

....

....

....

....

....

....

....

....

....

....

....

"The world is a prison for the believer and a paradise for the unbeliever." Muslim

These words carry insight, urging you to reflect on your perception of the world and your purpose within it. It's a game-changing reminder of the stark contrast in how Muslims and unbelievers experience this life.The notion of being a "prisoner", as portrayed in this hadith, signifies a life filled with meaning and self-control. It doesn't imply a life filled with limitations. It's not about being physically confined but about achieving peace of mind within the sanctuary of Islam.

As a believer, you might sometimes find this world a prison. Trials and tribulations, such as grief, illness, bullying, etc., can feel constricting, like heavy chains. But in these very challenges, lies an opportunity for growth, patience, and cleansing of sins.

Conversely, for the unbeliever, this world may appear as a paradise—a realm of individualistic indulgence and temporary selfish pleasures: pornography, sleeping around, and getting high on drink and drugs. Not caring about the consequences of their actions and refusing responsibility. However, it's crucial to remember that these pleasures are fleeting and do not lead to lasting contentment or success in the hereafter.

This world is flawed. It is not the soul's true abode. It's a temporary place where we face highs and lows. This life is a prison for the believer because the soul is away from its genuine home: paradise and Allah.

Contemplate these words deeply. Examine your own perception of the world—are you approaching it as a believer, recognising its trials as pathways to spiritual elevation?

....

....

....

....

....

....

....

Are you chasing momentary pleasures that lead to emptiness? May this reflection empower you to see the world through the eyes of faith, striving for the ultimate paradise that awaits in the hereafter.

....

....

....

....

....

....

....

....

....

....

"Indeed, in paradise, there are two gardens, their vessels and all that are in them are of silver. And, there are two gardens, their vessels, and all that are in them are of gold. There is nothing between the people and their seeing their Lord except the Cloak of Greatness upon his Face in the Garden of Eternity." And from the chain, it is reported from the Prophet (saw) he said: "Indeed in paradise, there is a great tent of hollowed pearl, its breadth is sixty miles, in every corner of it is a family, they do not see the others, and the believer goes around to them."
Tirmidi

Imagine a place of unimaginable beauty and splendour, where two gardens await you, one of silver and one of gold. These gardens are adorned with precious metals and filled with the most exquisite treasures that go beyond your wildest dreams.

But the true essence of jannah lies in what transcends its material beauty. Picture a scene where there is nothing between you and the sight of your Lord except for the Cloak of Greatness upon His Face. In the Garden of Eternity, believers will have the unparalleled privilege of gazing upon the Divine Countenance, an experience beyond compare.

And then, there is the magnificent tent of hollowed pearl, stretching an astonishing sixty miles in breadth. Within every corner of this vast expanse is a family, each in the company of their loved ones, basking in the glory of jannah. The beauty of it all is that they do not miss the presence of others, for their joy and fulfilment are complete.

Picture yourself as a believer, moving through this magnificent tent, meeting and rejoicing with your loved ones, and experiencing the sheer bliss of paradise. Dear sister, this is the promise that awaits those who strive in the path of Allah, who live their lives in obedience and devotion. It is a reminder of the boundless mercy and generosity of our Lord.

As we journey through this world with its trials and tribulations, let the vision of jannah inspire us to persevere and remain steadfast in our faith. May it fuel our determination to seek Allah's pleasure and guidance and to ultimately attain a place in the Gardens of Eternity. Indeed, jannah is more beautiful than we can imagine and is a reward beyond measure. May Allah grant us all His grace and mercy and guide us on the path leading to paradise's highest ranks.

Take a moment to meditate on the vivid description of jannah, as described by the Prophet Muhammad (saw). How does this description inspire and motivate you in your journey of faith?

"All who obey Allah and the Messenger, then they will be in the company of those on whom Allah has bestowed His Grace, of the Prophets, the steadfast affirmers of truth, the martyrs, and the righteous. And how excellent these companions are!" (4:69)

Among the shining examples of those who earned this sublime companionship, let me share with you the remarkable stories of two extraordinary women: Aisha and Khadijah. Imagine standing in the company of Aisha, the beloved wife of Prophet Muhammad (saw). Aisha was not just a witness to history but an active participant in transmitting the Prophet's teachings. Her youthful curiosity and profound wisdom have left an indelible mark on Islamic scholarship. Her dedication to learning and unparalleled knowledge of the Prophet's practices make her a role model for seekers of knowledge.

Now, picture yourself in the presence of Khadijah, the noble wife of the Prophet. She was a paragon of unwavering support and unwavering faith. Khadijah's strength during the early days of Islam, her selflessness, and her deep love for the Prophet Muhammad are an enduring example of what it means to stand by the side of righteousness, even in the face of adversity.

These women, Aisha and Khadijah, embody the essence of right-eousness and devotion. Their lives reflect the impact that faith, re-silience, and unwavering commitment can have on the path to righteousness.And remember, dear soul, if you obey Allah and His Messenger, you will be in the company of such luminaries in the hereafter. You will walk with the Prophets, stand shoulder to shoulder with the steadfast affirmers of truth, and share in the company of the martyrs who sacrificed everything for Allah's sake. The righteous will be your companions. So, let their light guide your way today.

As you journey through life, let this promise be your guiding star. Embrace obedience, seek righteousness, and know that Allah's promise is a radiant beacon illuminating your path, even in the darkest nights. In this world and the hereafter, you will find your-self in the most excellent company—a company that transcends time and space, a company of eternal excellence.

Imagine the blissful moment when, by Allah's grace, inshallah, you meet the Prophet Muhammad in jannah. What are the burning questions and heartfelt conversations you long to share with him?

....

....

....

....

....

....

....

....

....

....

In the gardens of paradise, you have the opportunity to meet the companions of the Prophet, both male and female. Among these remarkable companions, which female companion do you most yearn to meet, and what draws you to her?

....

....

....

....

....

....

....

....

Which male companion do you most yearn to meet, and what draws you to him?

....

....

....

....

....

....

....

"O Allah, I ask You for Paradise, and I seek refuge in You from the fire."

In the quiet moments of your heart, as you raise your hands in supplication, you have desires that are uniquely yours, aspirations that speak to the essence of your being. Let's explore two heartfelt supplications that you can make in your quest for the treasures of the hereafter.

Du'a No. 1: *"Allahumma inni as'aluka al-jannah wa a'oodhu bika min an-nar."*
"O Allah, I ask You for Paradise, and I seek refuge in You from the fire."

Imagine the depth of your longing as you utter these words. You're not just asking for paradise; you're yearning for a place where every moment is filled with joy and beauty beyond imagination. You're seeking an eternal home where your heart's deepest desires are fulfilled—where you will be surrounded by loved ones and where your soul finds lasting peace.

But you're also aware of your vulnerability, your humanity. With this supplication, you're acknowledging your need for divine protection. You're seeking refuge from the fire, the searing torment, and a path that leads to eternal suffering.

Du'a No. 2: *"Rabbana aatina fid-dunya hasanatan wa-fil akhirati hasanatan wa-qina 'adhaab an-nar."*
"Our Lord, grant us the best of this life and the best of the here-after, and protect us from the punishment of the fire."

In this prayer, you're not simply asking for worldly pleasures but seeking the best of this life. You desire a life filled with moments of happiness, love, and fulfilment. In this life, you can positively impact those around you. Your heart longs for a life of purpose, kindness, and gratitude. But your aspirations reach beyond the temporal. You yearn for the best of the hereafter—a place where your soul finds eternal happiness, every longing is met, and you are reunited with loved ones. You're asking for the ultimate success that transcends the boundaries of this world.

And as you make this dua, you're also beseeching Allah to protect you from the punishment of the fire, to guide you away from choices that could lead you astray, and to keep you on the path of righteousness.My dear sister, these duas are not just words but heartfelt expressions of your deepest hopes and fears. As you repeat them, remember that you are engaging in a profound conversation with the Divine—a conversation that has the power to shape your destiny and lead you to the treasures of jannah.

Reflect on the deepest desires of your heart and write down your most heartfelt dua to Allah.

....
....
....
....
....

What are the hopes and dreams that weigh heaviest on your soul?

....
....
....
....
....
....
....
....
....

My dear, consider the challenges you currently face in life. In light of these circumstances, what are the most fervent duas you wish to offer to Allah?

....
....
....
....
....
....

"Save yourself from jealousy. This is because jealousy consumes good deeds just as fire consumes firewood/ grass." Sunan Abi Dawud

My dear sister, let me share with you a powerful insight from the wisdom of our beloved Prophet Muhammad (saw). He spoke of a force that lurks within us, one that can silently erode our good deeds and tarnish our souls—jealousy. Visualise this: jealousy is a fire, an inner inferno that devours not the tangible but the intangible, not the body but the spirit. Just as flames consume firewood, jealousy devours your good deeds.

Now, consider this: our deeds are like precious gems crafted with love and sincerity. They are the glittering offerings we present to our Creator, the building blocks of our spiritual journey. But jealousy is a corrosive acid that eats away at these gems, leaving them diminished and disfigured. Jealousy blinds us to the beauty of our own blessings. It makes us resent others' successes as if their joy somehow diminishes our own. It taints our hearts with negativity, poisoning the well from which our good deeds flow. In a world that often encourages comparison and competition, it's easy to fall prey to destructive envy.

But my dear, you are better than that. You are a seeker of truth and a keeper of faith. To save yourself from the consuming fire of jealousy, remember this teaching. Guard your heart against envy, for it tarnishes the purity of your intentions. Celebrate the successes of others as a reflection of God's blessings, for their joy does not detract from your own. Instead of dwelling in jealousy, channel your energy into gratitude. Be thankful for the unique blessings bestowed upon you. Nurture a heart filled with contentment, knowing that your path is your own, and your journey is uniquely ordained. In this way, you can preserve the beauty of your good deeds and kindle a light that shines from within. As you navigate the world, let your heart remain free of the corrosive flames of jealousy, and your deeds will shine brighter in the sight of your Creator.

Girl, time to be honest with yourself, who are you jealous of?

....

....

....

....

....

Why are you jealous of them?

....

....

....

....

....

....

What is it that they have that you do not have?

....
....
....
....
....
....
....
....
....
....
....
....
....
....

Ponder this: Allah has given them unique blessings. But Allah has also given you special blessings. Whatever they have, it was written for them. It is their risq (provision). Would you like it if you knew some random girl was walking around having jealous, malicious thoughts about you?

....
....
....
....
....

. . . .

. . . .

. . . .

. . . .

. . . .

. . . .

. . . .

If there are people you follow online who make you feel envious or dissatisfied with your own life, it is a good idea to unfollow them. Take a moment to go through your Instagram and TikTok accounts and click that "Unfollow" button. If unfollowing will cause issues then mute them.

Here is a simple exercise you can do daily to cultivate a gratitude mindset: the 'Three Good Things' practice.

1. **Reflect**: At the end of each day, take a few minutes to reflect on your day's experiences. Think about three specific things that went well or made you feel grateful. These could be big or small, from major accomplishments to simple pleasures. For instance, you might reflect on having your senses, eyes that enjoy Allah's creation.

2. **Write Them Down**: write down these three things in detail. Be specific about why they made you feel grateful. For example, if you're thankful for having a healthy body, you

could write about how it allows you to take long walks in nature, play sports, or simply enjoy a pain-free day.

3. **Savour the Moment**: As you write down these three good things, take a moment to savour the positive emotions associated with them and thank Allah. Relive those moments in your mind, focusing on the joy, happiness, or contentment they brought you.

Make this a daily habit, preferably at the same time each day, like before bedtime or during your morning routine. Over time, this practice can shift your focus toward the positive aspects of your life and reduce your jealous thoughts. Try it now.

....

....

....

....

....

....

....

....

....

....

....

....

....

The Prophet (saw) said: "There is no believing servant who supplicates for his brother in his absence where the angels do not say, the same be for you." Muslim

This is your sign to do dua for not only the people you love but also those you hate or are jealous of. It's the ultimate heart cleanser. So, do wudu, roll out your prayer mat, raise your hands and make dua for three people you love and three people you can't stand. Trust me, you are going to feel so good.

....
....
....
....
....
....
....
....
....
....
....
....
....
....
....
....
....

Imam Bukhari relates from Mujahid, who said, "Ilm (sacred knowledge) is not gained by a shy person nor an arrogant one." Similarly, he relates from Aisha, who said, "How praiseworthy are the women of Ansar, shyness does not prevent them from having a deeper understanding of religion." Bukhari

You, my dear friend, stand at the threshold of sacred knowledge. But remember this: to unlock its treasures, neither shyness nor arrogance shall be your guide. In the wisdom of Mujahid, we find a truth echoed through the ages: Ilm, sacred knowledge, is a realm that shuns the timid heart and the haughty soul. It is a path that demands humility and a hunger for understanding. Look to the women of Ansar, who, as Aisha has praised, possessed a profound understanding of their religion.

Their example teaches us that shyness need not be a barrier to wisdom. So raise your hand and ask your questions. No subject is off limits because Islam has the answer to all your questions. Sometimes, we have to ask difficult questions to find out what is allowed and what is not for sensitive subjects such as intimacy, periods, puberty, etc. Alhamdulillah, there are many female scholars online whom you can reach out to. There are online courses as well. The sincerity of one's pursuit matters, not the volume of one's voice. So, my friend, step forward boldly but with a heart open to learning. Let neither shyness nor arrogance hold you back. Embrace the humility of a seeker, and you shall find that sacred knowledge is not a distant summit but a journey of continuous discovery.

Do I prioritise academic secular knowledge that leads to financial gain and career progression over acquiring Islamic knowledge? If so, how can I find a harmonious balance encompassing both aspects in line with my values and spiritual growth?

....

....

....

....

....

....

....

....

....

....

....

....

....

....

....

....

"Any Muslim who makes a supplication containing nothing which is sinful, or which involves breaking ties of relationship, will be given for it by Allah one of three things:He will give him swift answer, or store it up for him in the next world, or turn away from him an equivalent amount of evil." Mishkat al-Masabih

It's a simple truth that encapsulates the dynamics of supplication without needing embellishment. In its simplicity, it offers a glimpse into the immense mercy and wisdom of Allah. When you make a supplication, be mindful of its content. Let it be free from sinful intentions or actions that harm relationships. In doing so, you open the doors to three potential outcomes: Firstly, Allah may grant you a swift answer to your supplication, providing you with what you seek in this world. Secondly, He may store it for you in the next world, where the rewards are beyond our imagination. And thirdly, He may turn away from you an equivalent amount of evil, protecting you from harm and misfortune.

This wisdom isn't about the grandeur of words; it's about the sincerity of your heart and the purity of your intentions. It reminds you that every supplication you make is heard and has an effect, whether in this world or the hereafter. So, when you raise your hands in prayer, remember the simplicity of this truth. Let it guide you in crafting supplications free from sin and harm. Trust that Allah, in His infinite wisdom, knows what is best for you, and He responds to your heartfelt prayers in ways beyond your comprehension.

Considering the hadith that emphasises how Allah may respond to supplications, do you find it helps you understand why your duas are not always answered immediately?

....

....

....

....

....

....

....

....

....

....

....

....

....

....

....

How can you reconcile the culture of instant gratification in the modern world with the need for patience in your spiritual practice, particularly when you expect your supplications (duas) to be answered immediately?

....
....
....
....
....
....
....
....
....
....
....
....
....

What steps can you take to cultivate and develop patience?

....
....
....
....
....
....
....
....
....

Abu Hurairah said: The Messenger of Allah (saw) said, "Do you know what is backbiting? The Companions said: Allah and His Messenger know better. Thereupon he said, Backbiting is talking about your (Muslim) brother in a manner which he dislikes. It was said to him: What if my (Muslim) brother is as I say. He said, If he is actually as you say, then that is backbiting; but if that is not in him, that is slandering."

Imagine this: You're engaged in a conversation about someone, and your words take a turn that the person you're talking about would disapprove of. That, my dear sister, is backbiting. It's like speaking behind someone's back in a way they wouldn't appreciate. Now, consider this scenario: You're discussing another person, and your words accurately describe them. The Prophet's guidance here is a stark reminder. If your words match that person's reality, it's still backbiting. But if your words misrepresent them, if they go beyond the truth, that's not just backbiting; it's slander. This wisdom carries immense weight. It tells us that speaking ill of someone is a habit we should avoid, even if it's true. It's a stain on our character, a breach of trust, and a source of division among believers. We must be vigilant in a world (online and offline) where gossip and drama often run rampant.

Let's not succumb to the whispers of Shaitan and the allure of idle talk about our brothers and sisters. Instead, let our tongues be vehicles of kindness, wisdom, and truth. To speak well of others, to refrain from backbiting and slander, is not just a matter of words; it's a reflection of our character. It's a testament to our commitment to the bonds of brotherhood and sisterhood in Islam. As you navigate your path, remember this teaching from our Prophet (saw). Let your words be a source of healing, not harm. Let your conversations be filled with empathy and respect, for in doing so, you uphold the principles of our faith and preserve the unity of our community.

Do you find yourself in those moments with friends when the conversation swiftly veers into sharing stories about other women?

....

....

....

....

....

....

....

Now, picture for a moment that you're on the flip side of the coin. What if you discovered that your 'friends' are doing the same with stories about you? How would you feel?

....

....
....
....
....
....
....
....
....
....

It's a common habit that's easy to slip into.But girl, you can do better. The next time you're in that situation, consider gently steering the conversation in a different direction with a simple "Can we chat about something else?" It's your choice to foster more genuine and respectful interactions.

....
....
....
....
....
....
....
....
....
....
....

"Among His signs is the creation of the heavens and the earth and the diversity of your languages and your colours. Verily, in that are signs for people of knowledge." (30:22)

Let's dive right into one of the most beautiful aspects of our world: diversity. It's like a magnificent tapestry woven by the Divine, showcasing the richness of colours, languages, and cultures. Imagine you're in a bustling marketplace, where every corner represents a different region of the world. The vibrant tapestry of humanity is on full display – a breathtaking spectrum of skin tones and a symphony of languages filling the air. It's a scene that leaves you in awe, isn't it? Well, guess what? This diversity is no accident. It's one of the signs of Allah's greatness. A gentle nudge from the Divine, urging us to embrace and appreciate this colourful mosaic of humanity.

Islam stands firmly against racism, colourism, and nationalism. In the eyes of Allah, we're all equal, like different flowers in the same lush garden. It's not about where you come from or the shade of your skin; it's about the content of your character. Imagine a world where everyone looked and sounded the same – how dull would that be? It's the diversity of languages, colours, and cultures that makes our human experience so profound and beautiful. But here's the real gem: diversity is a sign of wisdom. When interacting with people from different backgrounds, you gain knowledge, broaden your horizons, and enrich your soul. It's like a lifelong adventure where every person you meet becomes a chapter in your story. So, savour the opportunity the next time you encounter someone from a different background. Embrace the chance to learn, grow, and celebrate the kaleidoscope of humanity.

When you encounter someone from a different background, take a moment to honestly assess your initial reactions.

....

....

....

....

....

....

Girl, be honest, do you find yourself making assumptions based on their appearance or accent?

....

....

....

....

....

....

....

....

....
....
....
....
....
....

We all carry stereotypes and biases, whether consciously or unconsciously. It's essential to challenge these stereotypes actively. Is there a negative stereotype that you hold about a particular group of people? Do you treat them differently because of it? Is that how you should be behaving as a Muslim?

....
....
....
....
....
....

Suppose elders in your family hold prejudiced views about other ethnic groups or compliment fair skin over darker skin. How can you tactfully advise them?

....
....
....
....
....

Abu Huraira reported that the Messenger of Allah (saw) said, "When one of you looks at someone who is better than him in wealth and physique, then he should look at one who is less well off than him." Sahih Muslim

Abu Huraira reported that the Messenger of Allah (saw) said, "Look at those who are beneath you and do not look at those who are above you, for it is more suitable that you should not consider as less the blessing of Allah." Sunan Ibn Majah

Picture this: You're scrolling through your social media feed, and there they are – those perfectly curated lives that seem richer, fitter, and altogether "better" than yours. Ever been there? Of course, you have; we all have. But here's the scoop from the Prophet Muhammad (saw): When you gaze at someone with more money or a seemingly perfect physique, take a step back. Look down, not up. Why? Because, my friend, it's all about perspective. The Prophet's wisdom hits hard with this gem. It's like a gentle reminder to shift your focus from what you lack to what you have.

Now, don't just nod and move on; let this marinate momentarily. Gratitude isn't about comparing yourself to those with more; it's about recognising and appreciating the countless blessings surrounding you. And here's another dose of wisdom: "Look at those who are beneath you and do not look at those who are above you, for it is more suitable that you should not consider as less the blessing of Allah." It's a double whammy of perspective adjustment.

Imagine flipping the script, recognising the blessings in your life, and celebrating them. That's where the true magic happens. It's like seeing the world through a new set of eyes. So, next time you catch yourself in the comparison game, remember these golden words. Embrace gratitude for the beautiful journey it is, filled with ups, downs, and countless blessings, tailor-made just for you.

By the way, I'm sure you're already aware that the vast majority of images you encounter online are heavily edited with filters to exaggerate reality. Many individuals extensively use image-editing tools, essentially 'face-tuning' themselves to an unrealistic degree. What you're seeing is far from reality, and it's crucial to remember that you can never attain these beauty standards because they're simply artificial. Girl, don't waste your time on this fake comparison game; you will never win; the odds are stacked against you!

Have you ever caught yourself measuring your worth based on the privileges someone else seems to have, whether in wealth or looks?

....

....

....

....

....

....

....

How did this comparison affect your self-worth and perception of privilege?

....

....

....

....

....

....

....

....

....

....

....

....

....

....

....

....

Abu Huraira reported Allah's Messenger (ﷺ) as saying,

"O people, Allah is Good, and He, therefore, accepts only that which is good. And Allah commanded the believers as He commanded the Messengers by saying: "O Messengers, eat of the good things, and do good deeds; verily I am aware of what you do" (23:51). And He said: "O those who believe, eat of the good things that We gave you" (2:172). He then made a mention of a person who travels widely, his hair dishevelled and covered with dust. He lifts his hand towards the sky (and thus makes the supplication): "O Lord, O Lord," whereas his diet is unlawful, his drink is unlawful, and his clothes are unlawful, and his nourishment is unlawful. How can then his supplication be accepted?" Muslim

If you desire your supplications to be answered, heed this stark truth: Obey Allah in how you lead your life. These are not just words; they are a reminder of the connection between your actions and the acceptance of your duas. The hadith paints a thought-provoking scenario, one that should prompt deep introspection. Your actions, your choices, and your lifestyle matter. To have your supplications answered, you must strive to live a life that is pleasing to Allah. Not a life that revolves around pleasing yourself or others, i.e. 'Doing what feels good'. When you raise your hands in prayer, let them be the hands of one who has embraced goodness in every aspect of life. Let your heart be filled with sincerity and devotion, for this is the path to ensuring that your supplications resonate with the acceptance of the Most Merciful.

Explore your mindset around dua (supplication): What beliefs or expectations do you hold when making dua?

....
....
....
....
....
....
....
....

Are there any doubts or uncertainties you've encountered?

....
....
....
....
....
....
....
....
....

Narrated by al-Tirmidhi describes how a man was leaving his camel without tying it. The Prophet (saw) asked him, 'Why don't you tie down your camel?' The man answered, 'I put my trust in Allah.' The Prophet (saw) replied, 'Tie your camel first, and then put your trust in Allah.'

This concise wisdom underscores a balance between reliance on Allah and taking practical measures. Yes, we put our trust in Allah, but we also have a responsibility to take practical steps and precautions in our lives.It's not about a lack of faith; it's about understanding that faith and action are not mutually exclusive. In fact, they complement each other. When you combine trust in Allah with the diligence of tying your camel, you create a powerful synergy. For example when you witness injustice, you do dua,

So, whether it's your career, your health, or your personal life, remember this lesson. Pray, have faith, and trust in Allah's plan, but don't neglect the practical steps and effort that are also part of the equation. Striking this balance is not a sign of weakness; it's a sign of wisdom. It's a testament to your understanding of the intricate interplay between faith and action. And it's a source of strength in navigating the journey of life as a Muslimah.

Consider a recent challenge or situation where you primarily relied on your abilities, perhaps forgetting to turn to Allah through dua. How did this approach work out for you, and in hindsight, could incorporating dua and seeking Allah's help have made a difference?

....
....
....
....
....
....
....

Reflect on how to strike a better balance between self-reliance and seeking Allah's guidance.

....
....
....
....
....
....
....
....
....
....
....

"And never will the Jews or the Christians approve of you until you follow their religion." (Al-Baqarah, 2:120)

As a woman of faith, you must recognise the importance of not seeking the approval and acceptance of non-Muslims, whether in the workplace, in friendships, or even in the course of dawah. Stay steadfast in your commitment to Islam without compromising your beliefs. This verse serves as a reminder that our faith is distinct, and the approval of others should never come at the cost of abandoning our core beliefs and principles. It's natural to desire acceptance and understanding from those around you. Still, it should always lead you to maintain your faith and values. Instead, strive to live as a proud and conscientious Muslimah, exemplifying the beauty of Islam through your character and interactions.

When doing dawah, focus on conveying the message of Islam with wisdom, compassion, and clarity. Invite others to explore the beauty of our faith, but do so while maintaining your own steadfastness in your beliefs. The strength of your conviction in Islam should be your guiding force. Your Islamic voice does not have to be quiet to soothe non-Muslim fears. It's not about pleasing others or seeking their approval but about upholding your faith's truth and principles. Why should you have to make your Muslim identity smaller to make others accept you? When you stand firm in your beliefs, you become a light, offering a clear and unwavering example of what it means to be a devout Muslim woman. So, stay true to your faith, and remember that Allah's approval is the ultimate goal. Doing so preserves your religion's integrity and inspires people to embrace Islam.

Why do I feel the need for acceptance from non-Muslims in various aspects of my life, such as at work, in social circles, or in educational settings?

....

....

....

....

....

....

....

What drives the desire to be accepted by those who may have different beliefs and values? Is it a desire for validation, a sense of belonging, or something else?

....

....

....

....

....

....

....
....
....
....
....
....
....
....

Recall a specific scenario at work where you faced a dilemma between pleasing non-Muslim colleagues to advance your career and staying true to your Islamic principles. How did you handle this situation, and what were the outcomes?

....
....
....
....
....
....
....
....
....
....
....
....
....

....
....
....
....
....
....
....

Think about a social gathering or event with non-Muslim friends where you encountered conversations or activities that contradicted your Islamic values. Describe how you balanced the desire to maintain those friendships with the need to uphold your faith. Reflect on any strategies or communication methods you used to convey your beliefs without alienating others.

....
....
....
....
....
....
....
....
....
....
....
....

In Sunan at-Tirmidhi, it says, "Allah loves to see the effects of His blessing on His slave." It was reported that Abul-Ahwas al-Jashami said the Prophet (saw) saw him wearing old, tattered clothes and asked him, 'Do you have any wealth?' I said, 'Yes.' He said, 'What kind of wealth?' I said, 'All that Allah has given me of camels and sheep.' He said, 'Then show the generous blessings that He has given you.'

This hadith isn't merely about flaunting one's material possessions; it's a reminder of gratitude and humility. Allah bestows His blessings upon us in various forms, whether it's wealth, health, knowledge, or influence over others. It's an acknowledgment of His benevolence, and it's our duty to recognise and appreciate these gifts.Showing the effects of Allah's blessings isn't about ostentation, but rather about using His gifts to benefit others, to contribute positively to society, and to express gratitude through acts of kindness and charity. It's about living a life that reflects the values of generosity, compassion, and gratitude.

As an intelligent Muslimah, you can internalise this wisdom and apply it to your own life. Whether it's the knowledge you've gained, the resources at your disposal, or the opportunities that come your way, use them to leave a positive impact on those around you. Let the effects of Allah's blessings shine through your character and actions.

In doing so, you not only fulfil your duty to express gratitude but also become a source of inspiration and goodness in a world that often needs it the most.

Think about the concept of "looking poor or unkempt" as it relates to Islamic dressing. Do you believe that being Islamic means you have to look impoverished or neglect your appearance?

....
....
....
....
....
....
....
....
....
....
....
....
....
....
....

Explore the idea that dressing well can also be an expression of self-respect and a means to present oneself with dignity as a reflection of your faith. How can you strike a balance between modesty and looking presentable?

....
....
....
....
....
....
....
....
....

What is your attitude towards dressing well and looking smart as a practicing Muslim? Do you feel conflicted between wanting to appear stylish and fearing that it might be seen as extravagant or materialistic in your faith?

....
....
....
....
....
....
....
....

....

....

....

....

....

....

....

....

Consider the hadith and teachings of Islam regarding moderation and balance in all aspects of life. How can you apply these principles to your approach to clothing and personal appearance?

....

....

....

....

....

....

Are there any changes you'd like to make in your wardrobe choices to align better with the concept of modesty and balance?

....

....

....

....

....

....

"O Mankind! We created you from a male and a female..." (49:13). Additionally, Allah clearly asserts that there are only two sexes in humanity: "...and from the two of them, He spread forth multitudes of men and women" (4:1), and "And the male is not like the female..." (3: 36)

There are only two genders, and you need not be swayed by the falsehoods propagated by liberal progressives. The objective biological evidence is crystal clear and readily available for anyone to check. Allah's guidance in the Quran reinforces this unambiguous reality. The divine decree underscores the fundamental binary nature of human creation.

Furthermore, Allah unequivocally asserts that there are only two sexes within humanity. The ayat reaffirms the intrinsic differences between the two genders as ordained by the Creator. In a crazy world where ideologies may attempt to blur the lines of gender, hold steadfast to the truth illuminated by your faith. The Quran provides unambiguous guidance grounded in the natural order of creation. Recognise and embrace the distinct roles and responsibilities assigned to each gender while treating all with kindness.

It's essential to remain grounded in the clear teachings of Islam, even when faced with societal pressures and contrary narratives.

Narratives based on personal feelings and no biological truth. Your faith provides you with the wisdom and clarity to navigate the complexities of the modern world while adhering to the fundamental truths laid out by your Creator.

How can I actively reduce the influence of movies, celebrities, and educational narratives about gender that do not align with Islamic principles or biological truths in my life and in the lives of those around me?

....

....

....

....

....

....

....

....

....

....

....

....

....

....

....

....

"This day, I have perfected your religion for you, completed My Favour upon you, and have chosen for you Islam as your religion" (Al-Maidah, 5:3).

G irl, you do not have to borrow ideas or views from capitalism, socialism, or feminism. Our faith, Islam, is a comprehensive way of life encompassing ethics, economics, social justice, and gender roles. It doesn't require us to adopt or borrow ideologies from other systems. In the Quran, Allah declares: "This day, I have perfected your religion for you, completed My Favor upon you, and have chosen for you Islam as your religion" (Al-Maidah, 5:3). These words convey a profound message. Islam isn't lacking in any aspect; it's a complete and perfected way of life.

You don't need to look elsewhere for guidance on structuring our lives, societies, or roles as women. Capitalism, socialism, feminism—each has its drawbacks. We just have to observe cultures that practice them, and we can see the problems. But none can fully replace the guidance provided by Islam. We have a rich tradition of scholarship, ethics, and values that guide us in navigating contemporary challenges while remaining rooted in our faith. So, embrace your identity as a Muslim woman with pride and confidence. You don't need to borrow from man-made, biased ideologies; you have a time-tested, divinely ordained path that offers guidance and solutions for today's and tomorrow's challenges. Your faith is a complete way of life, a source of strength in a world that often searches for answers in other ideologies.

Think about the common perception that society often presents Islam as merely a religion. Consider your own beliefs and experiences. Do you agree with this portrayal, or do you see Islam as a comprehensive way of life that encompasses not just spirituality, but also women's rights, economics, social justice, and more?

....

....

....

....

....

....

....

....

....

....

....

....

....

....

....

....

Society expects Muslim women to adopt a version of women's rights through feminism. Take a moment to reflect on your understanding of feminism and its core principles. Do you believe you know enough about feminist views to discern whether they align with Islamic values and teachings? If not start learning from Islamic people of knowledge who have studied Quran and hadith.

....

....

....

....

....

....

....

....

....

....

....

....

....

....

....

....

....

....

....

"An honourable man treats women with honour and respect, and only a despicable person treats women poorly." Suyuti

Dear sister, it is imperative to understand the honour and respect that Allah has bestowed upon you as a woman. This honour is not a mere social construct; it is a divine gift that you carry within you. No man or woman, no matter his or her station or authority, has the right to mistreat you emotionally or physically. Your worth, dignity, and right to be treated with respect are non-negotiable.

When we look at the Prophetic model, we find a beacon of guidance and compassion. The Messenger of God never raised his hand to strike a woman. He exemplified the highest standards of conduct, showing us that physical harm has no place within the bounds of a loving relationship. As narrated by his wife, the Prophet's advice to believers is clear and unwavering: *"The Messenger of Allah, peace and blessings be upon him, never struck anything with his hand, neither a servant nor a woman, unless he was fighting in the path of Allah." (Muslim)*

Consider the profound statement made by the Prophet: *"Would one of you beat his wife like a slave and then sleep with her at the day's end?!"* These words emphasise the absurdity of causing harm to the very person with whom you share your life, your joys, and your sorrows.

The Prophet's advice to believers is clear and unwavering: *Narrated Mu'awiyah al-Qushayri: I went to the Messenger of Allah (ﷺ) and asked him: What do you say (command) about our wives? He replied: Give them food what you have for yourself, and clothe them by which you clothe yourself, and do not beat them, and do not revile them." Abu Dawud.* These words are a testament to the importance of love, and kindness within the bonds of matrimony.

"Despite the Prophet's inherent distaste for harm towards women, there has been an attempt to argue for the permissibility of domestic violence based on an interpretation of a specific verse from the Quran (4:34). Contention ultimately arises on the issue of spousal abuse in Islam from a misreading of this particular verse. This verse states that if a husband fears his wife's egregious or defiant behaviour, he should follow a three-step procedure to solve the situation.

First, he must verbally advise her against her actions and correct her mistakes. If this does not improve the situation, he must then "abandon" her bed as a display of his disapproval. If that too does not prove effective, then the final measure has been translated as administering a symbolic gesture of physical discipline (*daraba*).

This multi-step procedure was arguably instituted as a means to regulate an initial surge of anger by requiring the husband to essentially cool down and not impulsively inflict harm upon his wife.

On initial reading of this verse, many readers tend to be frustrated with the ostensible permissibility of a husband hitting his wife. For this reason, scholars have discouraged laypersons from seeking legal answers from the Quran unguided as comprehension of the text requires expert interpretation and contextualisation. In fact, most Muslim sects agree that verses of the Quran can only properly be understood when read in light of other Quranic verses and the Prophetic model, as well as the interpretations and legal implementations of the scholarly elite. It was the scholars of each community who determined how this verse was not only understood, but what consequences could potentially follow if a husband wronged his wife in any way (i.e., physically or mentally).

In reality, the majority of scholars shared the Prophet's aversion to domestic violence and took measures to limit the apparent meaning of *daraba* or physical discipline in verse 4:34. According to the famous early Makkan jurist ʿAṭāʾ ibn Abi Rabah (d. 732 AD), *daraba* does not refer to hitting at all; rather, it is a symbolic gesture that reflects one's anger. He firmly contended, "A man does not hit his wife. He simply expresses that he is upset with her." Al-Darimi (d. 869 AD), a prominent early Persian scholar and the teacher of the two most renowned compilers of Prophetic narrations, Bukhari and Muslim, composed an entire chapter of hadith (Prophetic narrations) that objected to domestic violence titled 'The Prohibition on Striking Women.' Some scholars even went as far as challenging the authenticity of narrations that supposedly allowed men to hit their wives. Ibn Hajar, a scholar considered a medieval master of hadith, asserted that in spite of the apparent meaning of the Quranic verse, the example set by the Prophet is sufficient proof that hitting one's wife is reprehensible. The nineteenth-century Syrian jurist, Ibn Abidin, moreover, declared that any harm that left a mark on the wife could result in the physical punishment of the husband." Explanation from www.yaqeen.com_

My beloved sister, you are deserving of love, kindness, and respect. The teachings of Islam are a shield, a sanctuary. If you find yourself in a situation where these principles are violated, remember that seeking help is not just a right but a duty to yourself and your faith. Embrace the honour Allah has bestowed upon you, and let it guide you towards a life filled with love, respect, and dignity.

Start by acknowledging your inherent worth and value as a human being. I deserve to be treated with.......................................
....
....
....

....
....
....
....
....
....
....
....
....

If you or a loved one have experienced abusive behaviours, take a moment to list them. Whether verbal, physical or mental. Seeing them in writing can help you understand that these actions are un-acceptable.

....
....
....
....
....
....
....
....
....
....
....

....

....

Reflect on how this abuse has affected you emotionally, mentally, and physically. Consider the toll it's taken on your well-being and self-esteem.

....

....

....

....

....

....

....

....

....

....

Seek Support: write about the people who care about you, such as friends, family, or colleagues. Recognise that they would want you to be safe and happy.

....

....

....

....

....

....

....
....
....
....

Imagine a Healthy Relationship: Describe what a healthy, loving, and respectful relationship would look like to you. Compare this ideal to your current situation.

....
....
....
....
....
....
....
....
....
....
....
....

Overcome Fear: Explore the fears that are holding you back from seeking help. Understanding your fears can be the first step in overcoming them.

....
....

....

....

....

....

....

....

....

....

....

....

....

....

....

....

....

Build a Support Network: Make a list of people or organisations you can contact for support, such as family, friends, therapists or hotlines.

....

....

....

....

....

....

....

....

....

....

....

....

Set Small Goals: Break down the process of seeking help into manageable steps. Setting small goals can make the journey more manageable.

....

....

....

....

....

....

....

....

....

....

....

....

....

....

....

....

Visualise a Bright Future: Imagine a future where you are safe, happy, and free from abuse. Use this vision as motivation to take the necessary steps.

....
....
....
....
....
....
....
....
....
....
....
....
....
....
....
....
....
....
....

Do dua and ask Allah for strength and resilience. Repeat your duas daily to boost your confidence. Understand that seeking help is not a sign of weakness but courage and self-love—your well-being matters.Remember, you are not alone, Allah is with you. Seeking help is a brave choice that can lead to a healthier and happier life.

"How wonderful is the affair of the believer, for his affairs are all good, and this applies to no one but the believer. If something good happens to him, he is thankful for it and that is good for him. If something bad happens to him, he bears it with patience and that is good for him." Muslim

This saying is a mirror to the heart of a believer. It reflects the unshakable trust and resilience that comes with faith. It's not about the grandeur of words but the profundity of its meaning.For a believer, there's wisdom in all of life's experiences. When goodness graces your path, gratitude fills your heart, and that goodness multiplies. When adversity strikes: illness, grief, child loss, divorce, job loss, you embrace it with patience, knowing that within it lies a hidden wisdom and a chance for growth.

It's not about searching for the extraordinary; it's about finding the extraordinary within the ordinary. It's about recognising that your faith equips you to navigate life's twists and turns with grace and strength. This simple wisdom reminds you that, as a believer, every moment is an opportunity to draw closer to your Creator. Allah says: *"So, surely with hardship comes ease." (94:5)*. It's a reminder that goodness and hardship are intertwined, shaping you into a better version of yourself.

So, look for the ease when you are experiencing a difficult time. Embrace the simplicity of this truth. Let it guide you through life, and you'll discover that even in the simplest moments, there is opportunity to be content.

Think about a recent situation that made you feel deeply worried, especially when you realised it was beyond your control.

....
....
....
....
....
....
....
....
....
....
....
....
....

How did that experience affect your inner peace and well-being, and what did you learn from it?

....
....
....

....

....

....

....

....

....

....

....

....

....

....

....

....

....

....

Can you recall a time when you found yourself expending energy
and emotions on something you couldn't change or influence?

....

....

....

....

....

....

....

....

....

....
....
....
....
....

How would it feel to let go of such concerns, knowing that excessive worry often leads to negative outcomes?

....
....
....
....
....
....
....
....
....
....
....
....
....
....
....
....
....
....
....

Ibn Masood (ra) said that the Prophet (saw) said: "Among that which reached the people from the words of the earlier prophethood: If you feel no shame, then do whatever you wish." Bukhari

When you feel no shame, when you lose sight of the boundaries of modesty, you open the door to a world of moral ambiguity and recklessness. It's a stark warning against embracing a culture that promotes shamelessness and disregards the values that define your faith.

The Prophet's words don't restrict you; they free you from the shackles of heedlessness. They empower you to make choices that align with your values and your connection with Allah. They remind you that shame is a guardian of your soul, a compass that guides you away from actions that may lead you astray. Actions like being pressured into sending semi-naked selfies to guys or thinking it's ok to make money on OnlyFans. Just because lots of other women are doing it, it doesn't make it ok for you to do it.

So, let shame be your ally, your protector, and your conscience. It's not a weakness; it's a strength that keeps you grounded in your faith and morality. In a world that often confuses right from wrong, let these words resonate within you as a constant reminder of the importance of modesty and the path to righteousness.

You've astutely observed the changing landscape of society, one marked by increasing shamelessness in various aspects, including the sexual revolution and the LGBTQ movement. It's crucial to recognise that, as Muslims, we're guided by our faith and values, and we have the choice to uphold our principles in the face of societal shifts.

The prevalence of shamelessness in the public sphere does not compel us to accept or copy these ways of life. Islam provides a clear moral framework that emphasises modesty, self-dignity, and adherence to our beliefs. It's a reminder that we must stay strong in our faith and convictions, even when the world around us may seem to move in a different direction.

Our commitment to Allah's guidance, as conveyed through the Quran and the teachings of the Prophet Muhammad (saw), should serve as our compass in navigating these challenges. It's an opportunity to strengthen our faith, deepen our understanding of our religion, and engage in meaningful dialogue with those who may hold different views.

Rather than passively accepting societal changes, we can actively engage in conversations that promote understanding and respect for our beliefs. By doing so, we contribute to non-Muslim women finding out about the respect Allah tells women they should have for themselves. Women are not sex objects, our bodies are not their to be used by advertisers or ourselves to make a quick buck. If you don't respect yourself, why do you expect others to respect you?

Ultimately, our faith encourages us to be confident in our values while treating others with kindness and compassion. In a world where shamelessness may seem to prevail, our unwavering commitment to modesty and morality serves as dawah, demonstrating the beauty of our faith and the strength of our character.It's essential to acknowledge the seductive appeal of shamelessness that permeates society. Social media, dumb friends, fashion and beauty industry, all slowly chip away at our modesty.

Take a moment to reflect on instances where you've felt this pull and the impact it had on your values and actions.

....
....
....
....
....
....
....
....
....
....

....

....

....

....

....

....

Surrounding myself with individuals who share my values and principles is crucial. It's easier to resist societal norms when I have a support system that understands and respects my choices. How can I nurture and strengthen these relationships in my life?

....

....

....

....

....

....

....

....

....

....

....

....

....

....

....

Ali ibn Husayn reported the wisdom of the Messenger of Allah (saw) "Verily, among excellence in Islam is for a man to leave what does not concern him." Tirmidi

L isten closely, my dear: mind your own business. Resist the temptation to get entangled in juicy gossip or the affairs of others. You know how it feels when someone pokes their nose into your life, right? So, don't be a hypocrite.

Gossip and prying into the lives of others is destructive. It not only harms your relationships but also your own sense of integrity. By heeding this advice, you spare yourself from participating in hurtful behaviour. Just as you cherish your privacy and personal space, others do too. Respecting their boundaries fosters trust and genuine connections. Remember the golden rule: treat others as you want to be treated.

The tongue can be a double-edged sword. By avoiding unnecessary talk and gossip, you protect yourself from the harm it can cause. Remember that words can have a lasting impact. In essence, this wisdom is a call to practice mindfulness, honesty, and humility. It's a reminder that true excellence in Islam encompasses not just acts of worship but also how you conduct yourself in daily life. By leaving what does not concern you, you choose a path of dignity and respect—for yourself and others. Online, it's easy to be a nosy parker, treating privacy as dead. Her's an idea, instead of fixating on other people's lives, why don't you put your energy into improving your own life!

Begin by examining a moment when you've felt the urge to be nosy about someone else's life or affairs. Describe the situation in detail, including what triggered your curiosity and how you acted on it. Reflect on your motivations and feelings during these moments.

....

....

....

....

....

....

....

....

....

....

....

....

....

....

....

Recall a time when false rumours were spread about you. And then people did not bother to reach out to you for your side of the story. Instead, they placed their trust in a baseless online post, accepting it as the undeniable truth. Reflect on how this experience made you feel – the frustration, hurt, and the injustice of it all. Contemplate the impact it had on your relationships with friends and the sense of betrayal that might have lingered. This memory serves as a powerful reminder of the importance of seeking the truth and critically questioning the one-sided stories people tell you.

....

....

....

....

....

....

....

....

....

....

....

....

....

....

....

....

"Verily, Allah is gentle, and He loves gentleness. He rewards for gentleness what is not granted for harshness, and He does not reward anything else like it." Muslim

This beautiful hadith reminds us of a fundamental aspect of Allah's nature: His gentleness. It's a reminder that our Creator, the Most Merciful, appreciates and cherishes gentleness in our actions, words, and demeanour.But it doesn't stop there. The Prophet also tells us that Allah rewards gentleness in a unique way. He grants rewards and blessings for acts of gentleness that He doesn't grant for harshness. It's a powerful message about the effectiveness of kindness and patience in our daily lives.

So, what can we take from this hadith? It's a call to emulate the gentle nature of our Lord in our interactions with others. It's a reminder that when we respond to challenges, disagreements, or conflicts with gentleness, we're walking a path that aligns with Allah's own character. It's a way of inviting His blessings and, at the same time, fostering a more harmonious and compassionate world.

The next time you find yourself in a situation where you could choose between harshness and gentleness, remember this hadith. It's a beautiful reminder that the way of gentleness is not only pleasing to Allah but also a path to His unique rewards. May we all strive to be people of gentle hearts and kind actions, following the example of our beloved Prophet Muhammad (saw).

Imagine a moment where you felt the intensity of your own harshness, like a thunderstorm within your spirit. Take a breath and reflect. Who was the recipient of your sharp words or actions? What circumstances triggered this response?

....
....
....
....
....
....
....
....
....
....
....
....
....
....
....
....
....
....

Sulayman ibn Surad reported: Two people insulted each other in the presence of the Messenger of Allah (saw) and the eyes of one of them became red like embers and the veins of his neck were bulging. The Prophet said, "Verily, I know a word he could say to calm himself: I seek refuge in Allah from the cursed Satan." Muslim

This is a moment of guidance, a glimpse into the incredible wisdom of Islam. In times of anger and conflict, he taught us to turn to Allah, to seek refuge from the whisperings of Satan. Instead of fuelling the fire with insults and curses, take a pause, reflect, and let your heart be cleansed of hatred and bitterness. You see, my dear friend, cursing and insulting do not bring peace or resolution. They only serve to exacerbate discord and damage our souls. So, remember that as a Muslim, you should not engage in such behaviour.

On the topic of anger, here is some more advice. *Atiyyah reported: The Messenger of Allah, (saw), said, "Verily, anger comes from Shaitan, and Shaitan was created from fire. Fire is extinguished with water, so if you become angry, perform ablution with water." Abi Dawud*

"And come not near to unlawful sex (avoid all situations that might possibly lead to it.). Verily, it is a fahishah (immoral sin) meaning a major sin" (17:32)

These words are a stark reminder of the moral boundaries set by Allah, boundaries designed to protect your dignity, your faith, and your purity. They are a call to avoid even the faintest steps towards unlawful sexual relations, for it is a major sin, a grievous transgression.In a world where temptations are readily available and where moral values are often compromised, it's essential to heed this warning. Your faith and honour are at stake, and transgressing these boundaries can have profound consequences for your spiritual well-being.

Avoiding unlawful sexual relationships isn't merely about refraining from the act itself; it extends to looking, with desire at men, hanging out and being friends with non-mahrem men. Repeatedly doing this can easily lead to flirting, unwanted attention, sexual harassment or rape. It's a matter of guarding your modesty, protecting yourself, and preserving your integrity.Remember, obedience to Allah's commandments is a testament to your faith and your commitment to living a life that aligns with His guidance. It's a declaration of your determination to uphold the values that define you as a believer.

So, be vigilant in your choices and your surroundings. Don't just go with the flow. Surround yourself with friends who encourage and support your commitment to morality. And when faced with temptation, remember the words of Allah and the weight of this major sin, and let it serve as a shield to protect your heart and soul.

Take a moment to think about your personal safety and well-being. Have there been instances in the past where you felt uncomfortable or unsafe when becoming friends with men or being alone with them?

....

....

....

....

....

....

....

....

....

....

....

....

....

....

....

Explore your motivations and intentions behind your interactions with men. Do you want a companion? If you like attention from men but are not married, then this is your sign to start looking for a husband.

....

....

....

....

....

....

....

....

....

....

....

....

....

....

....

....

....

....

....

....

Finally, think about the steps you can take to ensure your safety while still engaging in healthy and respectful interactions with men. What strategies or guidelines can you implement to maintain your well-being without isolating yourself socially?

....
....
....
....
....
....
....
....
....
....
....
....
....
....
....
....
....
....
....
....
....
....

Aisha reported: The Messenger of Allah (saw) said, "Marriage is part of my Sunnah. Whoever does not act upon my Sunnah is not part of me. Give each other in marriage, for I will boast of your great numbers before the nations. Whoever has the means, let him contract a marriage. Whoever does not have the means should fast, as fasting will restrain his impulses." Sunan Ibn Mājah

Today, we find ourselves in a world where the concept of marriage and the allure of singledom, often influenced by Western ideals, have become subjects of concern. Let us reflect on this matter, bearing in mind the profound wisdom contained in the hadith.

In the Western world, there's a noticeable shift in the perception of marriage, with singledom often being glorified. It's imperative that we as Muslims hold steadfast to our faith and values in addressing this shift.

First, let us introspect. How do you, as an individual, perceive marriage? Is it a sacred covenant, a means of spiritual growth and companionship, or if you are married has it become a source of pain and hardship?

....

....

....

....

....

....

....

....

....

....

....

....

....

....

....

Moreover, consider the subtle influences of Eastern and Western ideas about dating, relationships, and commitment. These notions have the potential to infiltrate our beliefs. Have you, perhaps unknowingly, incorporated any of these ideas into your own thoughts on marriage? It is crucial to evaluate these influences in light of our Islamic principles.

....

....

....

....

....

....

....
....
....
....

If you've given up on marriage due to divorce or been delaying marriage, it's time to ponder the reasons behind your decision. Are you looking at failed marriages and believe that it's just not worth it?

....
....
....
....
....
....
....
....
....

Are your concerns legitimate, grounded in faith and wisdom, or have you succumbed to societal pressures that advocate postponing marriage? Remember, the hadith instructs that if you have the means, you should not delay in entering into the sacred bond of marriage.

....
....
....

....
....
....
....
....
....
....
....
....
....
....
....
....
....
....
....
....

Let us not forget the importance of embracing the guidance of our Prophet (saw). Parents, teachers and imams must encourage and facilitate marriage, making it an accessible and cherished choice for our Muslim brothers and sisters. We should not make marriages expensive ordeals. There also needs to be more support for divorcees and couples who are facing problems. Masjids should play a pivotal role in this. If you face problems in your marriage, seek help, speak to your family, you are not alone. May Allah guide you in your reflections and actions. Ameen.

"Fighting has been made obligatory upon you believers, though you dislike it. Perhaps you dislike something which is good for you and like something which is bad for you. Allah knows and you do not know." (2:216)

The verse acknowledges that going to war is not something most people naturally desire or find pleasant. Combat is brutal; fighting includes potentially being killed or wounded, striving against the enemies and enduring the hardship of travel. But Muslims are reminded of the 'good' that results from the fighting, i.e. justice for occupied people, freedom from slavery, liberation from colonisers, etc.

In his tafsir, Ibn Kathir says this ayah is general and not restricted to the topic of combat and warfare alone. You might love something, but it is not good or beneficial. Allah has better knowledge than you of how things will turn out and what will help you in this earthly life and the hereafter. Hence, obey Him and adhere to His commands so that you may acquire true guidance.

Explore the idea that the verse's message is not restricted to warfare alone. How does this broader perspective apply to your own life? Are there situations where you've desired something but later realised it wasn't truly beneficial for you?

. . . .

....

....

....

....

....

....

....

....

....

....

....

....

....

....

....

....

....

....

Contemplate the 'good' that can result from fighting, as mentioned in the verse. In what ways can combat lead to justice for oppressed people, freedom from slavery, and liberation from colonisers? Can you think of historical or contemporary examples that align with this concept?

....

....

....

....

....

....

....

....

....

....

....

....

....

....

Consider the notion that Allah possesses superior knowledge about the outcomes of events and what is genuinely good for us in this world and the hereafter. How does this idea influence your trust in divine wisdom and guidance?

....

....

....

....

....

....

....

....

....

....

"Tell the believing men to lower their gaze (from looking at forbidden things) and protect their private parts (from illegal sexual acts). That is purer for them. Verily, Allah is All-Aware of what they do."

"And tell the believing women to lower their gaze (from looking at forbidden things), and protect their private parts (from illegal sexual acts)" (24:30-31)

In the realm of faith, modesty and purity hold a significant place. Allah, in His infinite wisdom, has laid out guidelines for both men and women to uphold these values.

Lowering the Gaze: This guidance applies to both men and women. It encourages us not to indulge in inappropriate looks or stares that can lead to temptation or indecency. It is a reminder that we do not view each other as objects for our pleasure but as fellow human beings deserving of respect and dignity. By lowering our gaze, we preserve our own modesty and contribute to a culture of respect in society.

Protecting the Private Parts: Again, this rule is not gender-specific. It urges us all to safeguard our chastity and refrain from any sexual activity outside of marriage. By doing so, we uphold the sanctity of family and relationships in Islam, respecting the boundaries that Allah has set for our well-being.

It is not easy to follow these guidelines in a world saturated with hypersexualised content. However, the difficulty of the task should not deter us. Instead, it should inspire us, for the greater the challenge, the greater the reward in the next life.

These guidelines are not about restriction; they are about empowerment. They grant us control over our actions and decisions, protecting us from harm and ensuring our self-respect. Modesty is a source of strength, and purity is a reflection of our faith.In essence, these rules remind us of our worth as believers and the purity we should strive for in our interactions. They are a testament to our commitment to living in obedience to Allah's wisdom and ensuring our own well-being while fostering a culture of respect and dignity.

Do you find it difficult to not stare at men you find attractive?

....

....

....

....

....

....

....

....

....

....

....

Do you feel uncomfortable when men stare at you?

....

....

....

....

....

....

....

....

Take a moment to reflect and identify instances in your life when you catch yourself repeatedly staring at someone you find attractive. What circumstances contribute to this behaviour? If you want to marry them then speak to your wali/ mahrem and follow the sunnah. If not, you have to stop looking at them.

....

....

....

....

....

....

....

....

....

....

....

....

....

....

....

....

Now, consider what strategies you can employ to regain control
and redirect your gaze. Remember, you are in control of your actions. You do not have to act on every desire you feel. How can
you make a conscious effort to uphold modesty and respect?

....

....

....

....

....

....

....

....

....

....

....

....

....

....

....

Al-Nu'man ibn Bashir reported: The Messenger of Allah, (saw), said,"The parable of the believers in their affection, mercy, and compassion for each other is that of a body. When any limb aches, the whole body reacts with sleeplessness and fever." Muslim

When parts of our ummah are hurting, it extends across oceans and borders, transcending time and place. In occupied Palestine, occupied Kashmir, Yemen or among the Uyghur Muslims in China, when our fellow members of the ummah are in pain, the entire body should respond with heartfelt empathy, compassion, and action.

It is a matter that should awaken our collective conscience and move us to alleviate their pain.Inshallah, I pray that you are safe and not facing oppression, but imagine if you were. Wouldn't you want someone to help you, do dua for you, protest for you, collect charity for you, and raise awareness for the injustice you are facing? Posting on pro-Palestinian content has changed the way non-Muslims view the occupation of Palestine and Muslims are winning the narrative. Israel can no longer get away with their atrocities.This is all because of the actions of Muslims, Alhamdulilah!

I am writing this on the day the Zionist oppressors lay siege to Gaza. The despicable Muslim leaders and the west are not helping the innocent Gazans, but collectively, Muslims globally are doing everything in their power to help their brothers and sisters. We are unique, no other religious group loves each other as much as Muslims do. Artificial borders created by colonisers cannot divide us. Our ummah is not just a physical entity; it's a spiritual and communal bond, interconnecting us all. It signifies the unique bond of brotherhood that Islam fosters, reminding us that we are indeed one family, intricately woven together by our faith. We are not selfish or individualistic; we are selflessly connected, bound by a collective sense of responsibility and compassion.

Write a dua for your brothers and sisters facing oppression. If they were sitting next to you, what would you say to them to comfort them?

....

....

....

....

....

....

....

....

....

....

....

Abu Sa'id al-Khudri reported: The Messenger of Allah, (saw), said,"Whoever among you sees evil, let him change it with his hand. If he cannot do so, then with his tongue. If he cannot do so, then with his heart, which is the weakest level of faith." Muslim

This teaching imparts a crucial lesson about the responsibility we bear as individuals and as a community. When you come across something wrong, something haram taking place, something that goes against the Islamic values of righteousness and justice, you are called to take action.

The Prophet first advises us to change the evil with our hand, which signifies direct, physical intervention. If you are in a position to rectify a wrongdoing, do not hesitate to act. Use your hand to make a tangible difference, to uphold what is right and just.

But the reality is that we may not always have the physical means or authority to change the situation directly. In such cases, the Prophet advises us to use our tongue. Speak out against the wrong, raise your voice for justice, and use your words to rectify the situation. Silence in the face of injustice is not an option.

However, there may also be situations where using your tongue is not possible or effective, and that's where the final level comes in.

The Prophet tells us that if you cannot change the evil with your hand or your tongue, then at the very least, reject it in your heart. Do dua against the people committing the evil and do dua for the people facing the brunt of the evil. While this is the weakest level of faith, it's still a form of disapproval, a recognition that the evil goes against your values and beliefs.

In essence, my friend, this hadith teaches us that we must never be passive in the face of wrongdoing. Whether through direct action, verbal protest, or even within the confines of our hearts, we must actively resist evil and injustice.

How do you currently respond to instances of wrongdoing or injustice that you witness? Reflect on your actions and consider how you might align them with the wisdom of the mentioned hadith.

....
....
....
....
....
....
....
....
....
....

Dhurrah bint Abi Lahab reported: A man stood for the Prophet, (saw), while he was upon the pulpit, and he said, "O Messenger of Allah, who among people are best?" The Prophet said, "The best of people are the most to recite the Quran, the most fearful of Allah, the most enjoining of good, the most forbidding of evil, and the most to maintain family relations." Ahmed

My dear, let's unpack the profound wisdom encapsulated in these words. Firstly, the recitation of the Quran is the nourishment of our souls. The Quran is a source of divine guidance, and the more we immerse ourselves in its verses, the more we are able to navigate the complexities of life with the light of faith.Being among the best also requires a deep sense of taqwa, a consciousness and reverence for Allah. This consciousness nurtured by regularly reading the Quran.

Furthermore, we are encouraged to actively promote goodness and virtue, enjoining what is right and forbidding what is wrong. In a world that often strays from the path of righteousness, being among the best means setting a good example. We practice what we preach.

Lastly, cherishing family connections is another key aspect. The strength of the family unit is the foundation of a strong and harmonious society. By maintaining these bonds, we not only follow the sunnah but also contribute to the betterment of our communities. Enjoining the good and forbidding the evil is a vital aspect of Islamic ethics, and the extent of one's actions depends on their individual capability and circumstances. Here are some specific examples of how you can practice this principle within your means:

Offering Acts of Kindness: You can actively promote goodness by performing acts of kindness and charity. This might involve helping a neighbour in need, supporting a charitable cause, or donating to a food bank.

Promoting Virtue in Your Circle: Encourage good behaviour and discourage harmful practices among your family and friends. This might include advising against harmful habits like smoking weed, encouraging prayer, or promoting hijab.

Educating and Advising: If you have knowledge in a particular area, you can share it with others. For instance, if you are knowledgeable about Islamic finance, you can guide others in earning a halal income.

Being a Positive Role Model: Live your life in accordance with Islamic values. By being a positive role model in your conduct and character, you can inspire others to follow suit.

Dawah and Outreach: Depending on your skills and resources, you can engage in dawah and outreach efforts to address larger issues in your community or society. This might include volunteering and organising sisters circles or classes for youngsters.

You can use your social media accounts to do all of the above. Remember, that the principle of enjoining good and forbidding evil is flexible and adaptable to your personal capabilities and circumstances. It's about making a positive impact in your sphere of influence and contributing to the betterment of society within your means. Your actions may vary, but the intention to promote good and deter evil should always be sincere.

Which one of the suggested examples do you think you can put into practice?

....
....
....
....
....
....
....
....
....
....

The Messenger of Allah (saw) said: "We do not see for those who love one another anything like marriage."
Sunan Ibn Majah

irl, I know marriage is a hot topic! If you're tired of hearing about it, skip this section, if not read on. Marriage is not merely a contract; it's a sacred covenant. It's a union that goes beyond worldly bonds, a connection that transcends the physical. In a world where hookup culture often prevails, where fleeting encounters and casual relationships may seem tempting, remember the profound wisdom of our Prophet (saw). He reminds us that there is nothing that can compare to the depth and beauty of marriage.

Marriage is a sanctuary where love is nurtured, where two souls find solace in each other's company. It's a commitment that demands patience, understanding, and compromise. It's a journey filled with ups and downs, but therein lies its beauty.

However, it's essential to differentiate between love and lust. The allure of hookup culture often mistakes the temporary rush of physical attraction for the enduring warmth of love. Lust is fleeting, but love is steadfast. It's a bond that deepens with time and shared experiences.

Body count culture, where one's worth is determined by the number of past encounters, and casual hookups, is shaitan's quagmire. They often prioritise physical pleasure over emotional connection, leaving hearts empty and souls unsatisfied. These pursuits can lead to a cycle of emptiness, searching for fulfilment in all the wrong places.In contrast, marriage offers a different path. It's a commitment to building a life together, rooted in trust, respect, and genuine affection. It's a sanctuary where love grows, not diminishes.

In your experience, what distinguishes love from lust, and how can you ensure that you prioritise deep connections over shallow encounters in your own search for companionship and love?

....
....
....
....
....
....
....
....
....
....
....
....

"Women have rights similar to those of men equitably, although men have a degree of responsibility above them. And Allah is Almighty, All-Wise." (2:228)

Let Allah's guidance remind you that in His divine plan, men and women stand on equal ground when it comes to entering jannah. This equity is a testament to Allah's justice and wisdom. In your journey to jannah, never forget that you are entitled to rights, just as men are. These rights encompass all aspects of life – from your spiritual pursuits to your social and economic endeavours. Your faith acknowledges your intrinsic worth and ensures that you are treated with respect and dignity.

However, it's essential to recognise that while your rights are equitable, there exists a nuanced difference. Men bear a unique degree of responsibility that comes with its own set of obligations and duties. This distinction isn't a matter of superiority or inferiority but a divine order designed to maintain balance and harmony in society. As you navigate the intricacies of life, remember that your rights are firmly rooted in the teachings of Islam. They serve as a safeguard against injustice and inequality. Embrace these rights and responsibilities with a deep sense of purpose and faith.

The Sahabah understood 'rights similar' to mean the wife deserved the same compassion and kindness as the husband. This is why Ibn'

Abbas said, "Indeed, I spruce myself up for my wife, and she adorns herself for me, and I love that I should redeem all the rights I have over my wife so that she should redeem all the rights she has over me, because Allah (swt) said, "Wives have [rights] similar to their [obligations], according to what is recognised to be fair."

Allah has ordered that spouses should love and respect each other. Men, who are generally physically stronger than women, and they should use their strength to protect their wives, not dominate them. The Qur'an instructs men to *"Live with them in accordance with what is fair and kind."* (4:19)

Companionship is more than just paying for the household expenses or managing the home, although these are essential obligations. It is a higher objective that comes through intimacy and work. Needless to say, the Messenger (saw) stressed the importance to men, even if they possessed the most macho of qualities, to consciously reframe their relationship with their wives, *"The best amongst you is the one who is best to his wives, and I am the best of you to my wives." Reported by al-Haakim and Ibn Hibbaan on the authority of Aisha (ra).*

Today, gender relations have become a battleground with polarised viewpoints. One viewpoint trending is the "Red Pill" movement, which takes its name from the film "The Matrix." It is a social and political awakening, asserting that men are disadvantaged thanks to feminism. The "Incel" movement, short for "Involuntarily Celibate," claims that women have the upper hand, leaving men discriminated against. This movement is associated with misogynistic attitudes and condones abuse against women. Andrew Tate is the poster boy for the Red Pill movement. Even though he has become Muslim, he uses foul language against women, haram business practices, and promotes the privileges of manhood without its Islamic responsibilities.

But dismissing Tate as a sexist is not good enough, even though he is. Instead, his appeal should be seen as a sign of the real disorientation millions of boys and men feel. The symptoms can be seen in school, the workplace and family life. In the west, boys have fallen far behind girls in the classroom and on college campuses. Thousands of children are growing up without any relationship with their fathers. And in the UK and the US, every year, thousands of men commit suicide.

These trends result from the extraordinary successes of the women's movement. But it does prompt the question: what about the men? Many men feel disempowered without a clear direction of manhood. The old script for femininity, which valued marriage and motherhood, has been replaced with a new individualistic script for girls and women: you can do whatever feels good for you, and you don't need a man in your life to succeed. The old script for masculinity, where men had a role to provide and protect women and children, has also been tossed. But liberals haven't replaced it with a new, positive masculine script. That has created a dangerous cultural vacuum, one that figures like Andrew Tate are only too happy to fill and cash in on.

The Red Pill movement has also found currency in Muslim male spaces, with some young Muslim men adopting sexist and controlling attitudes. Factors contributing to this include competing with women for jobs, their marriage proposals being rejected and feeling their role as a husband and father is undervalued. This shift in values symbolises a departure from the tenets of Islam.

There's an acute need for Muslim fathers, imams, teachers, influencers and activists to condemn these movements. And promote the Prophet's example of love, mercy, and respect for women. Educating Muslim men on their history and highlighting that misogyny is not a part of Islamic tradition is crucial to moving forward as a community. It's time to untangle misogyny from Islam and establish women's rights based on Islamic principles, recognising men and women as equal believers. Initiating conversations centred on men's accountability and agency in addressing this problem is how to return harmony between the genders.

Always seek to uphold and obtain your rights with wisdom and grace, aware that Allah, the All-Wise, has ordained this equilibrium for the betterment of humanity. It's a balance that empowers you to fulfil your potential, contribute to society, and draw nearer to your Creator. In a world where the concept of rights can often be skewed or misunderstood, hold onto the clarity and wisdom of Allah's guidance. Your rights are a divine gift, and your responsibilities are a noble calling. Embrace them with strength, conviction, and unwavering faith.

Remember that the principles of feminism, although they may overlap with Islamic values in some aspects, are rooted in a secular and individualistic worldview. Before adopting any ideology, including feminism, it's crucial to research and critically evaluate its compatibility with your Islamic beliefs and values. Islam provides a comprehensive framework for women's rights, and Muslim women do not need to turn to secular ideologies to find empowerment and justice. And our communities must work harder to ensure women get their god-given rights.

Here are a few knowledgeable Muslim women I would recommend you follow online; they organise Islamic classes for women: Maryam Amir, Shaykha Dr Haifaa Younis, founder of jannahinstitute.org, Farhat Hashmi the founder of Al Huda institute and Fatima Barkatullah.

Do you know what your rights are as a Muslim woman, i.e. a daughter, sister, wife, mother, daughter-in-law, widow? What steps will you take to find them out if you don't?

....

....

....

....

....

....

....

....

....

....

....

....

Do you know what your responsibilities are if you are a daughter, sister, wife, mother, daughter-in-law, mother-in-law? What steps will you take to find them out if you don't?

....

....

....

....

....

....

....

....

....

....

....

....

....

....

....

If your rights are being taken away, who can you turn to for help? Remember you do not have to suffer in silence. Make a plan of how you will get help and support.

....

....

....

....

....

....

....

....

....

....

....

....

....

"The people of Paradise are lined up in one hundred and twenty rows. Eighty of them are from this nation, and forty are from the rest of the nations." Tirmidi

My dear soul, imagine this breathtaking scene shared by the Messenger of Allah, (saw). We get a glimpse of the hereafter's design and the blessings that await. Visualise a stunning display where the people of jannah are lined up in one hundred and twenty rows. Like a grand and harmonious assembly of souls, each one on a journey toward eternal joy.

Now, think about the incredible favour Allah has bestowed upon our ummah, our community of believers. Out of those one hundred and twenty rows, a remarkable eighty are reserved for the members of our blessed nation. This shows how Allah has generously welcomed those who held firm to their faith.

The remaining forty rows are open to the rest of the nations. This emphasises the wide-reaching mercy of Allah, reminding us that His compassion knows no bounds. This narration isn't just a story; it's a promise and an invitation. Inshallah, let it inspire you to strive with dedication and sincerity, so you may find your place among those who enjoy the highest ranks of jannah.

Abu Qatadah reported: The Prophet, (saw), said, "Verily, you will never leave anything for the sake of Allah Almighty but that Allah will replace it with something better for you." Muslim

There are many ways you can show commitment and devotion to Allah. These actions involve making choices that demonstrate your love for your faith.

Avoid Inappropriate Influencing: Refusing to participate in influencing that relies on your sex appeal (or your husband's good looks) and beauty for fame is an admirable decision. This could entail not dancing, singing or dressing modestly, using less makeup, and maintaining your dignity in your online presence. It's about choosing to prioritise jannah over popularity, freebies and cash. Making modest choices in your personal style and career decisions is essential. This means wearing the hijab correctly, rejecting trends that lead to immodesty, and turning down opportunities that conflict with your faith.

If you have a social media platforms that receive sponsorships for makeup and clothing, it may be challenging to maintain a balance between your faith and these sponsorships. Sacrificing could mean declining sponsorships that compromise your ability to speak about Islamic issues and injustice. It's a choice to prioritise your role as an advocate for Islamic values over financial gain. It may also involve refusing to promote movies or books that encourage feminism and promiscuity.

End a Haram Relationship: If you are in a haram relationship, such as having a boyfriend or an affair, making the choice to give up that relationship is a powerful decision. It's a testament to your love for Allah and your commitment to living by His guidance. It involves stepping away from a connection that gratifies you and you think is love but really it's just lust. If the guy you are involved with is unwilling to meet your family, tell his family about you and start immediately discussing marriage plans, how can you believe him when he says he loves you? You deserve better — a god-conscious man who wants a wife, not a girlfriend. Stop wasting your time. Don't jeopardise your jannah for a commitment-phobe.

Stop Smoking Cannabis: While it's important to acknowledge various approaches to relaxation and stress relief, it's crucial to understand that smoking cannabis is haram, as it alters one's state of mind similar to state of being drunk. It's advisable to explore alternative, halal methods for finding relaxation and managing stress. Engaging in regular prayer and dhikr provides a sense of inner peace and relaxation, allowing you to connect with Allah and find tranquility in your faith.It's essential to seek solace in practices and activities that align with the teachings of Islam and promote spiritual well-being, ensuring your journey is in accordance with your faith.

Leave a Haram Job: Opting to leave a job that involves haram activities or gaining income through interest is a significant act. This might entail walking away from a role where you buy or sell haram goods even if you aren't consuming it. Working for the police or army in the West, where you are upholding laws that contradict Islam. It could also involve leaving a workplace where you must wear a uniform that uncovers your arms or is figure-hugging or where you have to flirt with customers and socialise with male coworkers and clients to get a promotion.

Each of these decisions is an opportunity to draw closer to Allah and strengthen your connection with Him. Remember, Allah has promised that when you make these choices for His sake, He will replace them with something better, whether it's increased spirituality, peace of mind, or blessings in this life and the hereafter.

Is there a habit or aspect of your life that you find challenging to leave for the sake of Allah?

....

....

....

....

....

....

....

....

....

....

....

....

....

....

....

....

Write your dua to Allah asking for His help to overcome this challenge.

....

....

....

....

....

....

....

....

....

....

....

"Call upon Me, I will respond to you. Surely those who are too proud to worship Me will enter Hell, fully humbled." (40:60)

SubhanAllah! What a promise from the Creator of the heavens and the earth! He, the One who controls everything in this universe, is telling you that when you are facing hardship, when your heart is broken, call upon Him, He will answer your prayers.

Dua is the first step to making sense of your problems. You should get into the habit of making dua regularly. We all know the power and importance of prayers, but sometimes we forget. For those of us living in liberal, secular societies, it's evident that religion plays only a cameo role. It's pushed to the periphery of life and just makes a brief appearance during christenings, weddings, and Christmas.Unconsciously this mindset is influencing our thinking when it comes to making dua.

Over time, in liberal states, a societal shift occurred; the role of religion is accepted but as a benign instrument, not as a guide in all walks of life. We are feeling the cultural consequences of that shift, so we sometimes forget to make dua. How are we taught to solve our problems? By focusing on the supremacy of our individual talents and limitless potential. We are told to believe in ourselves, rely on our brainpower, skills, and knowledge. "You can do anything you set your mind to!" To rely on God is backward, old-fashioned, and unscientific. Unwittingly, we absorb these unrealistic ideas from popular culture and social media. But these empty slogans ignore our need for divine guidance.

There's more to this verse, my dear sister, Allah warns us about arrogance and pride. Those who turn away from His worship, those who refuse to humble themselves before Him, they will face a grave consequence. They will enter Hell, fully humbled.

You see, this verse is a powerful reminder of the importance of turning to Allah in humility and submission. We are nothing without Him, and we should never let pride and arrogance keep us away from His worship. When you call upon Allah, when you humble yourself before Him, He listens, and He responds. His mercy knows no bounds. *Abu Hurairah narrated that the Prophet (saw) said, "There is nothing more noble in the sight of Allah than dua" (Tirmidhi and Imam Ibn Majah).*

When you engage in dua, you display the utmost humbleness and accept that no one can assist you except Allah. Therefore dua is the essence of worship. Allah declares in the Quran: *Say (O Muhammad): "My Lord pays attention to you only because of your dua to*

Him. But now you have indeed denied (Him). So the torment will be yours for ever (inseparable permanent punishment)." (25:77)

In his tafsir of the above ayah, Qurtabi writes that Allah is telling us: "I have not created you because I have need for you, I have only created you so that you may ask Me, so I will forgive you and give you what you ask."

The Prophet (saw) said: *"Your Lord, may He be blessed and exalted, is characterised by modesty and generosity, and He is so kind to His slave that, if His slave raises his hands to Him, He does not let him take them back empty." (Abu Dawood)*

Ask Allah for whatever you want, as long as it is halal! Write you inner most desires.

....

....

....

....

....

....

....

....

....

....

"When God and His Messenger have decided on a matter that concerns them, it is not fitting for any believing man or woman to claim freedom of choice in that matter: whoever disobeys God and His Messenger is far astray" (Al-Ahzab, 33:36)

In the depths of your soul, dear sister, there lies a timeless truth —a sacred connection waiting to be acknowledged. It's a truth often overshadowed by the noise of the world, a connection that beckons you to align with the Divine's divine design. In a culture that champions self-will and personal choices, Islam brings a different message—a message of surrender, a path where submitting to the Divine leads to true liberation.

The verse from Al-Ahzab in the Quran is a radiant guide on this profound journey. It speaks of a beautiful bond, an intimate connection between Allah and His creation. It reminds us that when Allah and His Messenger have decreed a matter, it's not for any believing man or woman to assert their freedom of choice in that matter. This decree isn't a restriction; it's a gateway to divine wisdom and everlasting grace.

Understand that this submission isn't about oppression or suppression. It's about placing trust in the wisdom of the One who knows you better than you know yourself. It's about embracing a divine plan that transcends your limited understanding. In surrender, there's immense strength. In trust, there's profound empowerment. In submission, there's true liberation.

As you traverse the intricacies of life's journey, know that you're not solitary on this sacred path. Generations of believers have trodden this way before you, discovering solace and purpose in Allah's wisdom. It's a shared voyage where hearts unite in devotion, and souls find their eternal sanctuary. So, when the world tempts you with distractions and divergences, when it urges you to abandon the path of surrender, cling to the wisdom of this verse. In His guidance, discover a love unparalleled.

Take a moment to ponder how we have been conditioned to hate the idea of obedience to Allah, but obeying our feelings and desires is celebrated.

....
....
....
....
....
....
....
....
....

Mu'adh ibn Jabal reported: The Prophet (saw), said, "The people of Paradise will enter Paradise with smooth and hairless skin, kohl upon their eyes, at thirty or thirty-three years of age." Tirmidi

The hadith paints a portrait of the people of paradise. Picture the radiant souls entering the gardens of eternal bliss, their skin unblemished and smooth, akin to the finest silk. Imagine their eyes, adorned with kohl, shining with a light that surpasses our earthly understanding.But this narration is not merely about aesthetics; it is about the spiritual essence that transcends time and space. The smooth skin is a reflection of purity, free from the scars of sin, a soul cleansed by faith and good deeds. The kohl on their eyes is not just adornment but a testament to the depth of their inner vision, the clarity with which they saw the truth.

As we contemplate their age, at a tender thirty or thirty-three years, we see a reminder of the eternal youth and vitality of the heart. It is a reminder that in paradise, time is a concept that no longer restricts or defines us. We remain forever in our prime, unburdened by the limitations of age. Dear friend, let these words inspire you to embark on a journey of inner purification, to seek a heart that is unblemished by sin, and a vision that is adorned with the clarity of faith. Inshallah, you can be a person of jannah.

"All of you are shepherds, and every one of you is responsible for his herd... a man is the shepherd over his family, and a woman is a shepherd over her husband's house and children." Al-Bukhari and Muslim

In the words of our beloved Prophet Muhammad (saw), dear sister, lies a shared responsibility of guardianship among all believers. It's a divine trust, a role that calls upon each of us to be a shepherd, guiding and nurturing those under our care.

Consider the analogy: "All of you are shepherds." In this statement, the Prophet encapsulates a significant message. A shepherd is not merely a passive observer but an active guardian—a protector and guide. In your life's journey, you, too, are entrusted with a flock. For a man, it's the stewardship of his family, while for a woman, it's the honour of overseeing her home and children.

This responsibility is not a burden; it's a sacred duty. It's a recognition of the vital influence you possess within your sphere of guardianship. As a woman, you hold a powerful pivotal role—a role that shapes the moral and spiritual landscape of your household.

Embrace this role with pride and purpose. Your influence as a guardian is instrumental in nurturing faith, instilling values, and fostering love within your family. It's a partnership, a beautiful interdependence between husband and wife, where each complements the other's strengths, working together to steer the family towards righteousness.

Remember that your blood sweat and tears are recorded by the angels. Your love, faith, and dedication are the compass guiding your family's hearts. Your home is not just a physical space; it's a sanctuary from haram influences. In the contemplation of why the roles of wives and mothers have been undervalued, it is vital to recognise the influences of both capitalism and feminism, which have contributed to and promoted a negative view of this essential work.

Capitalism, with its emphasis on economic productivity and profit, has had a significant impact on how we perceive and value work. In a capitalist society, economic success and the pursuit of wealth often take precedence over other forms of labour. This can lead to the devaluation of roles that are not directly associated with monetary gain.

In this framework, unpaid domestic labour is often overlooked and under appreciated, as it does not contribute to the gross domestic product or generate income. While feminism has been instrumental in opening up opportunities for women in the workforce and empowering them to pursue careers, it has contributed to the devaluation of the work of wives and mothers. In the process of advocating for women's rights in the workplace, there has been a tendency to equate success and fulfilment solely with external achievements, often at the expense of recognising the valuable contributions made within the home.

In the quest for a more equitable and inclusive society, it is essential to acknowledge and appreciate the multifaceted nature of work and the value of all roles, inside the home and out. Redefining success and worth beyond monetary terms and recognising the invaluable contributions made within the home are important steps toward a more balanced and just societal perspective.

So, my dear, when you ponder the words of the Prophet Muhammad (saw), understand that you're entrusted with a noble task. Your role as a shepherd within your home is a testament to your strength and wisdom. Embrace it with grace, recognising the impact your guidance can have on the generations that follow.In this shared guardianship, find unity and purpose. In nurturing faith and love, discover the path to a harmonious and blessed household. Your role is not merely one of duty; it's a sacred journey of nurturing hearts and souls.

Have you ever felt like the work of a homemaker often goes unnoticed and under appreciated?

....
....
....
....
....
....
....
....
....
....

Do you find it to be the case that working women are granted greater respect compared to those who choose to stay at home?

....
....
....
....
....
....
....
....
....
....
....

Are you be pressured to go out to work when you would rather stay at home? After all it is not your duty to pay the bills, that is the role of the husband.

....
....
....
....
....
....
....
....
....
....
....
....
....
....

Do you think women who work are overly criticised. Whether they are single or married.

....
....
....
....
....
....

Nowadays, the norm is that both husband and wife work. Both must pay attention to their responsibilities in the family. And rather than argue; it's essential to speak to each other and work together to build a tranquil home. If you feel your efforts are not valued, or you feel like you are doing two jobs, jot down your worries and choose a calm moment to talk to your husband about your concerns. That's how you can bring about change. Don't allow resentment to fester.

....

....

....

....

....

....

....

....

....

....

....

....

....

....

....

....

....

Al-Bayhaqi reported: Hamdun al-Qassar, may Allah have mercy on him, said, "If one of your brothers commits an error, seek seventy excuses for him. If your hearts do not accept it, know that the fault is with yourselves." Shu'ab al-Imān 10436

In the treasury of our faith, a pearl of wisdom gleams brightly – the practice of thinking the best, not the worst, of your fellow Muslim, extending seamlessly into the digital realm of our interconnected world.

Imagine a scenario: you stumble upon an online story or rumour concerning a Muslim. Photos, video clips, screenshots of conversations. The information is sensational, perhaps even shocking, and you're tempted to assume the worst immediately. But in the spirit of thinking well of others, consider an alternative approach.

Now, imagine that a friend, perhaps someone you don't particularly like, comes to you with a juicy piece of gossip about someone you know. They claim that this person has done something to hurt them, and they eagerly share their side of the story.

In both of these scenarios, it's crucial to maintain a balanced perspective. Resist the urge to rush to judgment or to form negative conclusions prematurely. Instead, keep an open heart and mind.

Approach your fellow Muslims, whether face-to-face or online, with empathy and a commitment to thinking the best.

He (saw) also said "*A Muslim is the one from whose tongue and hand, (other) Muslims remain safe.*" *(Ahmed)*

Engage in open and compassionate dialogue, as our beloved Prophet Muhammad (saw) encouraged. Reach out to those involved, express your concerns, and seek clarification regarding the story's authenticity. By doing so, not only do you prevent the spread of fake news, and one-sided gossip, but you also manifest your dedication to maintaining unity and understanding within our community. Imagine the lies were being spread about you, how would you feel? After all lying is a grave sin.

Narrated Abu Huraira: The Prophet (ﷺ) said, "Whoever does not give up false statements (i.e. telling lies), and evil deeds, and speaking bad words to others, Allah is not in need of his (fasting) leaving his food and drink." Bukhari

Embracing the virtue of thinking the best enables you to nurture the bonds of brotherhood and sisterhood, even when confronted with the challenges of misinformation in the digital age. In a world where AI can generate life like pictures and clone voices, screen shots can be edited, you can no longer believe what you see. People lie, hold grudges, they have evil intentions so don't get dragged into their drama.

"Don't nurse grudge... A Muslim is the brother of a Muslim. He neither oppresses him nor humiliates him nor looks down upon him. The piety is here, (and while saying so) he pointed towards his chest thrice. It is a serious evil for a Muslim that he should look down upon his brother Muslim. All things of a Muslim are inviolable for his brother in faith: his blood, his wealth and his honour/ respect." Sahih Muslim

Holding grudges does more harm to you than anyone else. When you cling to anger and resentment, that bitterness becomes a poison that eats away at your soul, darkening your heart. Girl, let go of grudges, and discover the liberating power of forgiveness. Understand that when you forgive, you're not condoning the wrong that was done to you, but rather freeing yourself from the chains of hatred. Forgiveness is an act of self-love; it's a gift you give yourself. It lightens your heart and paves the way for healing and growth.

Think of the beautiful example set by Abu Bakr, the beloved companion of the Prophet Muhammad (saw). When his relative, Mistah, slandered his daughter Aisha, it was a deeply painful moment for him. But he didn't let that pain fester into grudges or hatred. Instead, he chose the path of forgiveness and reconciliation.

By forgiving Mistah, he did not look down on him, Abu Bakr demonstrated a level of magnanimity that not only reflected his character but also earned him the praise of Allah. For on the Day of Judgment, it is said that Allah will forgive those who have shown forgiveness to others. I'm not advocating you become a doormat. Learn from your dealings with immoral people, you don't have to let them back into your inner circle. But, by forgiving, you pave the way for Allah's forgiveness in return on the Day of Judgment.

I am going to forgive and let go of the grudge I am holding on to

....

....

....

....

....

....

....

....

....

....

....

....

....

....

....

....

The Prophet (saw) said:"Convey from me even if it is (only) one ayah." Bukhari

Calling people to Allah's guidance (dawah) is a vital and glorious mission. It means inviting people to worship Allah alone, bringing them on from darkness to the light, planting goodness in the place of evil and truth in the place of falsehood. Islam is the fastest growing religion, we want people to join our family. Alhamdulilah, Muslims are the most welcoming people. When you do dawah you are following in the footsteps of the prophets.

When doing dawah, do so with knowledge and gentleness. Allah says: "*Invite (humankind, O Muhammad) to the way of your Lord (i.e. Islam) with wisdom (i.e. with the Divine Revelation and the Quran) and fair preaching, and argue with them in a way that is better. Truly, your Lord knows best who has gone astray from His path and is the Best Aware of those who are guided." (16:125)*

Allah also says:
"*And by the Mercy of Allah, you dealt with them gently. And had you been severe and harsh-hearted, they would have broken away from about you; so pass over (their faults), and ask (Allah's) forgiveness for them; and consult them in the affairs." (3:159)*

Calling people to Islam brings great rewards. *The Prophet (saw) said: "Whoever calls others to guidance will have a reward like the rewards of those who follow him, without that detracting from their reward in any way. And whoever calls others to misguidance will have a burden of sin like the burden of those who follow him, without that detracting from their burden in any way." Muslim*

So imagine that a person becomes Muslim or a Muslim returns to Allah thanks to you taking the time to speak to them. Or you post Islamic content or because you authentically represent Islam. Inshallah, you will share in the rewards of their good deeds.

Which friends could you start speaking to about Islam. What issue s do they care about? Environment, poverty, women's rights? Research what Islam has to say about the issues so next time they talk about it you can gradually show them the Islamic perspective, inshallah maybe their interest will be piqued, remember dawah is not debating or arguing. It's an invitation.

. . . .

. . . .

. . . .

. . . .

. . . .

. . . .

. . . .

Rifa'ah al-Juhani reported: The Messenger (saw), said, "I testify before Allah that no servant dies bearing witness there is no God but Allah and Muhammad is the Messenger of Allah and then does what is right, except that he will find his way into Paradise. My Lord Almighty has promised me that seventy thousand of my nation will enter Paradise without reckoning or punishment. Verily, I hope you will not enter Paradise until all of you settle together in the heavenly residences with your righteous forefathers, your spouses, and your progeny." Ahmed

As you reach the final hadith of this book, you find yourself in the company of a great soul, Rifa'ah al-Juhani, who has shared with you a timeless message from our beloved Prophet Muhammad (saw). What a fitting way to conclude our journey together, with the promise of paradise he brings you.

The Messenger of Allah (saw) declares, "I testify before Allah that no servant dies while bearing witness that there is no God, but Allah and Muhammad is the Messenger of Allah and then proceeds to live a righteous life, except that he or she will find their way into Paradise." This testimony, my dear reader, carries the weight of eternity, and the Prophet Muhammad was the bearer of glad tidings, a mercy to you and all of humanity, chosen by the Almighty.

"My Lord Almighty," he continues, "has promised me that seventy thousand of my nation will enter Paradise without facing the trials of reckoning or the agony of punishment." This, indeed, is the boundless mercy and grace of your Creator.

But what makes this a perfect note to end your journey is the Prophet's aspiration. As part of the ummah, he wishes for you to gather in Paradise not as isolated souls but as a united community. Picture this, Allah says in a hadith qudsi: "*I have prepared for My righteous servants what no eye has seen, what no ear has heard, and what no heart has perceived.*" *Bukhari.* A celestial gathering, where you reunite with your righteous forefathers, cherished spouses, and beloved children. This is the promise of a community of believers bound together by the profound testimony of faith.

In these words, find hope and faith, my dear reader. Strive for righteousness, bear witness to the Oneness of Allah, and follow the guidance of the Messenger. Through this, you may hope to join that blessed company in Paradise, where the joy of reunion awaits and the mercy of the Most Merciful envelops you.

As you close this book, remember and carry these words in your heart. May you live by this testimony and enter Paradise as a united community, as the Prophet (saw) envisioned. It is a promise of everlasting boundless love that awaits you.

ABOUT THE AUTHOR

Farhat Amin is an author & host of the podcast, her books include Smart Teenage Muslimah, Smart Single Muslimah, Hands Off Our Hijab and Child Loss, Bereavement & Hope. She has delivered lectures & courses on Women in Islam and feminism. She shares life advice that is Islamic and honest thought-provoking via her website www.smartmuslima.com. Where you can enrol in her Pre-marriage Course For Muslims, and Sex Education for Muslimahs.

Her aim is to help women achieve confidence in their faith. The inspiration for both her website and podcast is Surah Asr:

"By Time. The human being is in loss. Except those who believe, and do good works, and encourage truth, and recommend patience."

She felt there was a need for a platform that represents Muslim women without falling into the temptation of watering down Islam for the sake of mass appeal. As Islam encourages hikmah (wisdom) when informing others of Islam, not compromise.

Printed in Great Britain
by Amazon

37780141R00108